Team
Power

Team Power

How to Build and Grow Successful Teams

Jim Temme

SkillPath Publications
Mission, KS

We have acknowledged the sources of all activities, research studies, and other information, factual or anecdotal, contained in this book to the extent we were able to identify them.

Editor: Kelly Scanlon

Page Layout: Premila Malik Borchardt and Rod Hankins

Cover Design: Rod Hankins

ISBN: 1-878542-93-1

Library of Congress Card Catalog Number: 96-68230

10   9   8   7   6   5   4   3   2   1   96   97   98   99   00

.

Printed in the United States of America

Contents

Preface

An underlying priority in writing this book on team building is to provide readers with a comprehensive reference to guide them in the development and growth of teams. Information abounds about building teams and instilling a sense of teamwork. Much of it seems too theoretical or fragmented. This book will guide you through all the important issues of building and sustaining a *real* team.

Unfortunately, there's too often a "rush" to hurry up and get teams in place. You really can't rush the behavior changes necessary for effective team building. These include such behaviors as building trust, motivating team members, understanding and positively handling conflict, tactfully giving performance feedback, coaching, counseling, empowering team members and encouraging them to accept responsibility.

Likewise, you can't rush skill building. There are a number of skills that team leaders and team members must learn and continuously practice. Some of these include goal setting, effective planning, getting results, solving problems, making decisions, and conducting meaningful team meetings.

The book will take you through an educational journey about all of these behaviors and skills and more. You will learn that teams go through stages of development and that these stages, too, can't be rushed. Also, you will learn the value of understanding personality styles and differences. If team members can understand their differences in personality, they can rise above them.

Finally, the last chapter of this book, "Staying the Course," will give you a template or step-by-step model for building a solid team. It is a guideline, a road map you can use to aid the team-building process. You don't necessarily have to follow each step precisely. Teams develop differently and at different rates of speed. But the model will help you to stay focused.

The title of this book, *Team Power: How to Build and Grow Successful Teams,* reflects the whole process of sharing control with the team and giving the team the power to influence its own outcomes. Developing a team is about understanding the skills and behaviors needed to help the team accomplish goals and objectives and get results. Growth is about continuous learning and helping team members to reach their potential. Growth is about maturity.

This book will help you on your journey to effective team development, whether you're just starting out or have gotten lost along the way and need to find the road back to success. Best of luck to you and your team as you pursue the joy of working together!

Acknowledgments

This book is dedicated to two people I value very much in my life: Jim Chohrach and Tom Mahaffey, former supervisors I had the privilege to work for. They taught me what it really means to be a team leader and a team player. They exemplified key life traits that have lighted life's path for me so I could keep moving forward in my journey. From them, I learned the value and meaning of compassion, commitment, hard work, thinking before speaking, listening to others, empathy, leading by example, trusting in others, being a friend, giving without expecting anything in return, and encouraging others to believe in themselves.

Unfortunately, they both left much too soon. I will remember them always and I dedicate this book about "togetherness" to them. Your shining example has given me the wisdom to write this book.

What Makes a Team

What Is a Team?

In their rush to jump on the team-building bandwagon, many top corporate executives are sending out mandates to their staff to get teams up and running and to do it within a very short period of time—like three months.

The mandate itself is an irony. Teams aren't supposed to have mandates imposed on them. They are supposed to be *a part of* the planning and decision-making process. And of course, being *involved* in this process is what empowerment is all about.

This leads to one definition of a team: *A group of people who have been empowered to set goals, make decisions, and solve problems and who have the commitment to make changes to implement their goals and decisions.*

Let's elaborate on the key words in this definition.

Empowerment is simply the sharing of power. This means that a team must not only be given responsibility for outcomes, but also must have the authority to produce those outcomes.

Goals are absolutely essential to a team's success. In fact, a team is not really a team if it has no goals. Goals are the glue that holds the team together. Without them, instead of a team, you simply have an assembly of people who work together, which is really just a work group working under a new label called "team."

"Teamwork is the ability to work together toward a common vision. The ability to direct individual accomplishment toward organizational (goals and) objectives. It is the fuel that allows common people to attain uncommon results."

—Author Unknown

Another key word is *commitment*. If the team members aren't committed to the goals and to each other, goals likely won't be accomplished. What makes team members commit to goals? More than anything else, it is *participation!* The team, with the help of upper management and team leaders, must be allowed and encouraged to define its own destiny. This assistance from formal authority figures is called *coaching*. (This will be discussed in greater detail in Chapter 6.)

Yet another key word in the team-building definition is *change*. The very nature of team building requires change. People are asked to support, rather than to compete, against each other. Managers are asked to share their power rather than withhold it. Team members are asked to take on a different type of responsibility than they may be used to. In the beginning, the change can be disconcerting to everyone involved. People are being pushed out of their comfort zones. Yet one of the most important and beneficial aspects of team building is to make a change for more efficient business operations, better products and services, and enlightened people, all of which results in improved quality.

The Relationship of Teams to Total Quality

Much of corporate America's interest in teams over the last decade has been associated with the Total Quality Management movement. In and of itself, TQM is often a target of criticism and skepticism. In fact, some managers think TQM stands for "time to quit and move on."

"Team spirit is what gives so many companies an edge over their competitors."

—George L. Clements

However, if implemented properly, TQM can have far-reaching positive effects on a company and its personnel. But in order to have Total Quality Management, there must first be total management quality!

Total quality management *is the continuous improvement of goods and services, procedures, and people ultimately to serve customer needs more effectively.*

For continuous improvement to have an impact rather than just be a rallying cry, there must be input for improvement from all levels in the organization. Many of the companies that have successfully implemented TQM have consequently formed work teams to solve customer problems, to improve products and services, to make decisions on how to proceed, and to continuously train team members. Total quality management and team building, therefore, go hand in hand.

The late Dr. W. Edwards Deming, who gets much of the credit for the TQM concept and who particularly assisted the Japanese in implementing it, explained that in order to continuously improve, it is important to involve your most important business assets— the employees. After all, they must know something. They are building the products and providing the services. It only makes sense then to involve them in creating the future.

"The race for quality has no finish line."
—Often quoted phrase

Types of Teams

Building a team can sometimes be confusing because there are so many kinds of teams in the workplace. Here's an overview of some of them:

- **Quality circles.** These were popular in the early 1980s in the United States; they were the forerunners of improvement teams. Team members made suggestions for changing procedures and on improving products and services. However, they weren't usually vested with much authority to make and finalize decisions. They just passed their recommendations on to upper management. Notice that they are discussed here in the past tense. They aren't common anymore, in part because they had little authority.

- **Improvement teams.** In many workplaces today, teams exist to improve particular processes, products, or services. These teams have replaced quality circles as a more common type of team. The difference is that they not only make recommendations, they are also empowered to make decisions, often in concert with managers outside of the team. In other words, there is a collaborative effort between team members and managers to arrive at decisions together.

  Generally speaking, improvement teams aren't permanent. Once they accomplish their improvement goals and tasks, they disband. In some instances, if the team performs admirably, team members continue to work together to solve other improvement problems. These are sometimes called *project teams*.

- **Work teams.** "Work teams" is a rather generic term. Here, it means a team organized around a function or group of functions. For instance, what is often called a department, such as the accounting or personnel department, will change its name from the accounting department to the accounting team. The idea of the name change is to reflect a change in the work culture. That is, to get employees to rethink their "functionality" or the way they do business, namely, to take more responsibility for problem solving and decision making.

Often, for example, employees who performed only one function will learn multiple functions. This is called *multiskilling* or *cross training*. Team members learn to work with and support each other. They are empowered by the team leader, who may well be the supervisor of the "department." The traditional supervisor becomes the "team coach." Rather than telling people what to do, the coach guides and assists people to make decisions, solve problems, set goals, and take action. Work teams are usually permanent since their functions are ongoing in the organization.

- **Self-directed work teams.** As their name implies, these teams have reached a point of maturity where they can be self-managed. Self-directed work teams (SDWTs) usually start out as work teams or, possibly, as improvement teams. Team members reach a high level of trust with each other and with the supervisor or coach.

The important word here is *trust*. Trust develops because team members continually follow through on goals and tasks. The team has proven that it has earned the right to be self-managed, and leadership from within has begun to occur.

This process generally can take two to five years. Once teams have reached this point of maturity, they can begin to select their own leader, set their own goals, do their own scheduling, define their own budgets, conduct peer performance reviews and do their own employee selection. This is still a somewhat radical concept in many companies. For SDWTs to work requires managers who, themselves, have

"Quality is not an act. It is a habit."

—Aristotle

a strong self-concept and who don't feel threatened by empowering others. Also needed are employees who aren't afraid to get out of their comfort zone to take risks and assume personal responsibility for outcomes.

Because the development of SDWTs is challenging—moving towards SDWTs requires both patience and persistence—they don't work in every work environment. But those organizations that are up to the challenge and have the patience to see the concept through can expect real rewards in terms of greater creativity and heightened productivity.

Figure 1 is an "empowerment continuum." It displays the relationship between various kinds of teams and the role of management. The extreme left on the horizontal line indicates strong management control and authority. At the other end of the continuum is team control and authority.

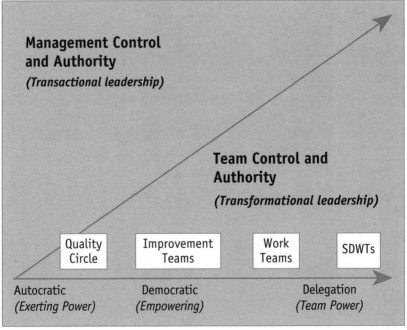

Fig. 1. *The empowerment continuum.*

The extreme left of the continuum is sometimes called "transactional leadership." It reflects the idea that managers give employees work to do. In exchange, the employees receive a paycheck and, sometimes, health and other insurance benefits. Unfortunately, some managers make the assumption that employees work only for a paycheck and that staff members are concerned only about themselves. Management assumes that if everyone receives a paycheck, productivity will rise.

The right side of the continuum represents the concept of "transformational leadership," which suggests that employees and managers will be transformed by the empowerment process. Managers learn that employees will ultimately take more interest if they are involved in their own outcomes and if they have the opportunity to participate in problem solving and decision making. Managers learn that real power comes from respect. Employees are more likely to respect managers who help them grow and who are supportive of them rather than those who condemn and use power over them.

Employees learn that taking responsibility for decisions and outcomes can be exciting and meaningful, particularly if their supervisor supports them. Once employees learn that they can trust their supervisors to stand behind them, employees learn that it's all right to push past their comfort zones and to take risks. When creativity is encouraged, it prospers—and both the employees and the organization are transformed.

"Always do right. This will gratify some people and astonish the rest."

—Mark Twain

The Key Traits of a Real Team

Calling a team a team does not necessarily mean that it really is one. A team must act like a team day after day.

The characteristics that make a team successful has been the subject of many studies and much research. Tom Peters and Robert Waterman, Jr., in their watershed book *In Search of Excellence* and Patricia Gallagan, who has written extensively on the subject for the *Training and Development Journal* (American Society for Training and Development) are only a few of the researchers who have gathered extensive data on what it takes for a team to be successful. Here are some of the key traits of effective teams.

1. **Trust.** For a team to grow and prosper, team members must learn to trust each other. *Actions speak louder than words.* It's not what people say they're going to do, it's what they do that counts. If team members are consistent in their words and follow through, then trust will develop. If people are consistently inconsistent, then it's unlikely that team members will learn to trust one another. Employees must live up to their commitments in order to be trusted. The same thing is true for a leader who wants to be trusted by team members.

2. **Empowerment.** As discussed earlier, the team needs to be vested with responsibility and given the power to influence outcomes. Without authority to make decisions and solve problems, a team is really just a work group under the label of a team. Team leaders must be willing to share power, and—just as important—team members must be willing to assume the responsibility that comes with being empowered.

3. **Authentic participation.** Participation goes hand in hand with empowerment. Authentic participation must be genuinely encouraged. The common term for authentic participation is "job intimacy," which means that team members can speak up and act without fear of reprisal.

Without authentic participation, a real team doesn't exist. Instead, you have a work group composed of people who speak up only when it's safe or when they feel they will be in agreement with the boss. Some people call this "politics." A better term is "group think." "Team members" realize that making suggestions and being creative will only get them into trouble, so there's no authentic participation.

Authentic participation, then, is one of the most important and successful traits of a real team. It results from leadership that truly encourages open communication and rewards people for their ideas rather than condemning them.

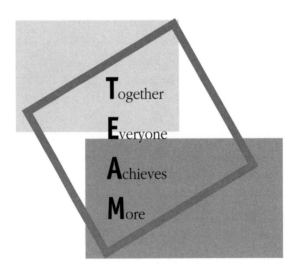

Together

Everyone

Achieves

More

4. **Ability to manage conflict.** Conflict is good! Through their differences, team members can arrive at better decisions. If team members are willing to share their perspectives through open communications and fellow team members are willing to listen and be nonjudgmental, then the team is likely to have a "synergistic experience." Synergy is the concept that the sum of the parts is greater than their individual effects. Or, put simply, two heads are better than one.

Unfortunately, when ideas are presented, disagreement often supersedes listening and understanding. Team members can begin to compete against each other for the best idea. An "I win-you lose" mentality can develop. Instead of mutual support, unhealthy competition develops.

In conflict management, the goal is to strive for a "win-win" solution. That doesn't mean that the team will always get one, but it's always worth striving for. Conflict resolution is discussed in more detail in Chapter 12.

5. **Basic communications skills.** One definition of communication is that the other person gets the same message you sent, or conversely, you receive the same message that the other person intended. If team members all have different perceptions of what they are supposed to do, how it is to get done, who is to do what, and what the deadline dates are, the team likely has a communications problem.

To resolve communications problems, team members must concentrate on giving each other useful feedback that ensures communication has really occurred. One of the biggest communication problems is assuming that communication has occurred. By using feedback, the team can continually monitor communications.

6. **Use of delegation to help others learn**. On effective teams, leaders delegate important tasks so that team members can learn and take responsibility. Motivational studies consistently point out that employees want challenging work. On a team, members should be carrying out the important goals and tasks, and team coaches should be guiding progress through effective coaching and feedback.

7. **Willingness to embrace innovation, creativity, and risk taking.** On a real team, these actions are encouraged. As discussed earlier, a team is more likely to be innovative and creative if there is open communication and authentic participation. Risk

taking also plays a major role in the creative process. If the team has creative ideas and arrives at innovative solutions to problems, it must be willing to test its conclusions. Unfortunately, however, this is often the point at which a team becomes immobilized.

The team leader and team members must be willing to risk making mistakes and failing occasionally. The French philosopher Collette said, "You will make mistakes, but make them with enthusiasm." When Thomas Edison was asked about his life success, his response was, "I failed my way to the top." The former ice hockey goalie Jaques Plante put it a little differently. He said, "How would you like it when every time you make a mistake a big red light goes on and ten thousand people boo?"

While people shouldn't be encouraged to make mistakes, it's true that implementing creative, innovative ideas carries the risk of failure. However, it more importantly means that the team is likely to succeed and prosper through new and useful ideas.

8. Leadership. A team needs solid direction. As it applies to a team, leadership is related to effective coaching and counseling. Coaching implies providing direction and giving assistance to team members so they can succeed. Counseling means listening to team member ideas, concerns, and needs and helping team members take responsibility to meet their own needs.

"Experience is what enables you to recognize a mistake when you make it again."

—Earl Wilson

Leadership, then, is not only accomplishing team goals and purposes, but also helping team members grow and prosper in the process. Or, stated another way, leadership is directly related to empowering team members to become the best they can be. The Chinese philosopher, Lao Tzu said: "The superior leader gets things done with very little motion. He imparts instruction not through many words but through few deeds. He keeps informed about everything but interferes hardly at all. He is a catalyst. And although things wouldn't get done as well if he weren't there, when the group succeeds he takes no credit, and because he takes no credit, credit never leaves him."

9. **Decision-making skills.** Team members must be encouraged to make decisions. Remember the definition of Total Quality Management: continuous improvement of goods, services, procedures, and people ultimately to serve customers more effectively.

Another way of saying it is that TQM is related to meeting customer needs through effective problem solving. To solve problems, a team must arrive at creative, innovative solutions. It must then *decide* on the best solution and act!

10. **Integration of personalities.** Teams often are most successful when team members complement each other. For instance, one person on the team may be very detail-oriented, whereas another may concentrate more on the big picture. Some team members may be people-oriented, while others might want to concentrate on the tasks more than interrelate with people. Differences in personality also bring a variety of perspectives and strengths to the team.

11. Need for constructive change. The key word here is *flexibility*. Companies and individuals who are aware of changes going on around them and who can adapt to and make timely changes are likely to continue to grow and prosper.

But people have a tendency to resist change because it pushes them out of their comfort zones. Anything new and different brings with it the possibility of failure. Thomas Ferranda, in a book called *Uncommon Sense*, pointed out that "what used to be isn't anymore and what is won't be for long." We live in a constantly changing world or, to put it another way, the only constant in life seems to be change. Teams need to be constantly aware of the need to change in order to compete effectively.

12. Goals and objectives. A team is not a team unless the team members have a common purpose. As mentioned earlier, goals are the glue that holds the team together. One of the common mistakes management makes in team building is to assemble a group of people, call them a team, and then charge individual team members with doing the same things they were doing before they became a team.

Goals answer the question, "What are we going to do?" Objectives answer the question, "How will we get it done?" Team members take on responsibility to carry out the goals and objectives. Ultimately, what the team has is a plan of action and a commitment to succeed. Commitment comes from the team being empowered to define its own goals and objectives with the assistance of the team coach. Notice the word *assistance*. A common mistake is for the team leader to decide for the team what its goals will be. Teams need to be actively involved in their own outcomes.

13. Training. Real teams get training. Companies and organizations that commit to team building must also commit to training. Team members are being asked to work differently than the way they did previously. Because they're expected to make decisions and solve problems, team members need to be trained about effective problem solving and decision making. They need to know about conflict management and personality styles. Team members need continuous training to be continually enlightened about the need to work effectively together.

In particular, teams should be trained to continually focus on these thirteen key traits and to analyze their progress. Team members need to know how to handle conflict, solve problems and make decisions, deal with change, learn how to communicate, and understand what it means to be a real team.

The end-of-chapter exercise will help you and your team assess your progress in building a real team. It is important to involve your team in determining your success in team development.

> *"We work day after day not to finish things; but to make the future better ... because we will spend the rest of our lives there."*
> —Charles F. Kettering

Measuring Your Team's Success

Team Effectiveness Grid

Instructions: Place an X on the grid on the scale from 1 to 10, indicating where your team is functioning in relation to each trait listed below. At the bottom of the grid, list additional traits (e.g., reward system, role identity, profitability, emphasis on quality, having fun, effectiveness of meetings) that you would like to measure. Again, rate how you feel your team is doing in regard to each trait you add. Connect the Xs together to give you a profile.

	1	2	3	4	5	6	7	8	9	10
Trust level										
Empowerment										
Authentic participation										
Managing team conflict										
Communication skills										
Delegation skills										
Innovation, creativity, risk taking										
Leadership										
Decision-making skills										
Integration of personalities										
Encouraging and handling change										
Goals and objectives										
Training										
Other traits unique to our team:										

Team Effectiveness Grid

(Team Exercise: Have your team complete the exercise.)

Instructions: Place an X on the grid on the scale from 1 to 10, indicating where your team is functioning in relation to each trait listed below. At the bottom of the grid, list additional traits (e.g., reward system, role identity, profitability, emphasis on quality, having fun, effectiveness of meetings) that you would like to measure. Again, rate how you feel your team is doing in regard to each trait you add. Connect the Xs together to give you a profile.

	1	2	3	4	5	6	7	8	9	10
Trust level										
Empowerment										
Authentic participation										
Managing team conflict										
Communication skills										
Delegation skills										
Innovation, creativity, risk taking										
Leadership										
Decision-making skills										
Integration of personalities										
Encouraging and handling change										
Goals and objectives										
Training										
Other traits unique to our team:										

Analyzing Your Team's Results

Answer the questions below to assess your results.

1. What is your total effectiveness index? _____ (Add your scores for each trait. A top team performance would be a score of 91 or better. This is an average score per trait of at least 7 [13 x 7 = 91]. If you listed additional traits that you wanted to evaluate, then add 7 points per trait to arrive at a top performance score.)

2. What two categories did you rate the highest?

   _____

   _____

3. Why did you rate these the highest?

   _____

   _____

4. What two categories did you rate the lowest?

   _____

   _____

5. Why did you rate these the lowest?

   _____

   _____

6. Indicate how you will follow up to deal with the categories you rated the lowest. It is important to start dealing with weaknesses with haste. As a suggestion, it is a good idea to involve your team in finding ways to make improvements.

   _____

   _____

Using the Results to Make Team Improvements

How you and your team use the results from the Team Effectiveness Grid is important. Don't use it to criticize or manipulate the team in any way. Use it to help your team validate its strengths and weaknesses and develop an action plan to make changes for improvement. Here are some tips to consider as you analyze the results.

1. **Focus on total results, not individual scores.** For instance, if you have ten people on your team and nine of them rate the clarity of goals and objectives at seven or above, that's an indication that the team is fairly successful with this trait. If only one person rates goal clarity at one or two, then it's unlikely that score is valid. Look at the overall average.

2. **On the other hand, do look at the mode—how many times the same score appeared for a given trait.** For instance, on a team of ten, there could be five people who rate clarity of goals and objectives as a ten and then another five who rate goal clarity as only a one. If that's the case, then there is validation that at least half your team sees a problem with that trait, which means you and your team do need to question the strength of that trait.

3. **Tackle problems quickly.** When you use the Team Effectiveness Grid, your team members will want to know the results quickly. Then they will expect that problem areas will be discussed and remedied reasonably soon.

"There is nothing more difficult to take in hand, more perilous to conduct, or more uncertain in its success than to take the lead in the introduction of a new order of things.

—Niccola Machiavelli, The Prince

4. **Solicit members from the larger team to form a small "improvement team" that focuses on developing ideas to improve the team.** For instance, if goal clarity is a concern, the improvement team would begin defining ideas to handle this problem. In some instances, you can have several improvement teams of three or four people, each of which works on a specific trait the instrument targeted for that improvement.

5. **Be sure to let team members know where the scores were high!** For instance, if the instrument shows that the team scored high in handling change, let everyone know that's generally how the team sees itself. Continue to focus on behaviors that encourage acceptance of and implementation of change.

6. **Focus on problems, not people.** One of the basic tenants of Total Quality Management is that most problems are "systems related." Unfortunately, though, when something goes wrong, people will often point fingers and place blame. A systems problem is an underlying problem that needs to be solved in order to eliminate the real cause.

   Here's a good example of a systems-related problem: An employee in a fast-food restaurant is blamed for holding up the line because she's not filling orders fast enough. On the surface, it appears that the employee is either lazy, unmotivated, or unintelligent. When the the manager reviews the problem in greater depth, she discovers that the equipment used to prepare the food is outdated and malfunctioning. No matter how much the employee is blamed, criticized, or even motivated, she won't be able to do her job until the real (systems) problem is fixed.

"Keep the Line Moving Forward"

The main point is to follow up on the survey results. Keep people informed. Communicate! Fix problems and weaknesses. Keep moving forward in your pursuit of quality team building to get quality results. This is referred to as "line control."

Have you ever been to one of the major theme parks? When you stand in the line, it keeps moving forward until you get to the front. If you're always moving, you perceive that you're making progress. But on the highway when there's an accident, you feel stressed if you are going nowhere. If a lane of traffic opens, even if you're only going five miles an hour, you feel like you're making progress. The idea is that you're moving forward. You are making progress.

Thus line control in team management is related to the idea that you should always keep moving or progressing toward improving your team and getting results. In other words, you are striving for continuous improvement. Effective team leaders keep team members focused on results and success!

"Perseverance is a great element of success. If you only knock long enough at the gate, you are sure to wake up somebody."

—Henry Wadsworth Longfellow

2

Team Chemistry: Social Stages of Development

The Stages of Team Development

Do teams automatically gel? Do team members automatically trust each other?

In a word, no—or at least rarely. To build a real team takes hard work and attention. Teams that work have likely passed through several stages of development before trust really developed and before team members really began to gel with each other.

For a team to successfully accomplish its goals and get results, a synergy must develop between team members themselves and between team members and the coach or supervisor. The four stages that a team goes through to reach synergy are:

- Defining
- Planning
- Follow through
- Transformation

> *"I'm just a plowhand from Arkansas, but I have learned how to hold a team together. How to lift some men up, how to calm down others, until finally they've got one heartbeat together, a team. There's just three things I'd ever say:*
>
> *If anything goes bad, I did it.*
>
> *If anything goes semi-good, then we did it.*
>
> *If anything goes real good, then you did it."*
>
> —Paul "Bear" Bryant

These parallel the "Tuckman Model," whose stages are often referred to as forming, storming, norming, and performing. Figure 2 depicts the growth and development of a team as it moves through the various stages. Notice that as a team moves closer to the transformation stage, there is greater team control and authority and less management control and authority.

Let's look now at the behaviors that accompany each stage. It's important to note that even team members who are used to working with each other may revisit these stages each time they set a new goal.

- **Defining (forming).** A successful and effective team should have a clear idea of what it wants as an outcome. One of the big mistakes supervisors and companies make in their quest to form teams is to assemble a group of people but give them

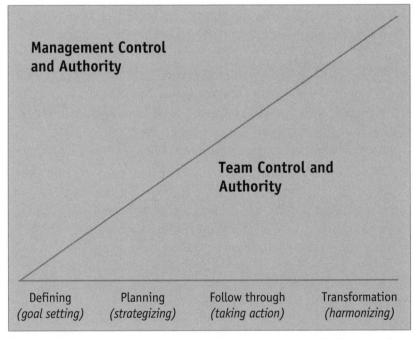

Fig. 2. *Stages of team development and corresponding level of team and management authority.*

no focus. Team members become frustrated because they don't see any purpose for forming teams. They continue to do the same things they were doing before. They just have a new label called a team.

The supervisor or team coach is responsible for getting the team to focus on results right from the start. But to get results, the team needs to know what it will do. With the assistance of the coach, the team can define its goals. Then the team members will have a clear focus. They can be goal-focused and results-oriented.

Another vital role the coach plays is helping team members get to know each other so they can become familiar with each others' skills and talents.

- **Planning (storming).** After a new team knows what it wants to accomplish, it can start focusing on "how" to get it done and who will do what. At this stage, the team leader needs to assert his or her coaching ability, particularly with a newer team.

Team involvement is essential at this point, so the team leader elicits the feedback of team members about how to accomplish their goals and tasks. Of course, there will likely be disagreements, so conflict is likely to erupt. Thus, this stage is often called the "storming" stage.

Conflict in and of itself is good because it leads to multiple solutions to problems and different ways to accomplish goals. Unfortunately, however, if the conflict isn't resolved, then it becomes destructive. The team leader needs to keep team members concentrating on resolving differences to arrive at agreed-upon methods for accomplishing team goals. Figure 3 shows the process of strategic planning that will keep the team moving forward.

"Make your enemy your friend."

—English proverb

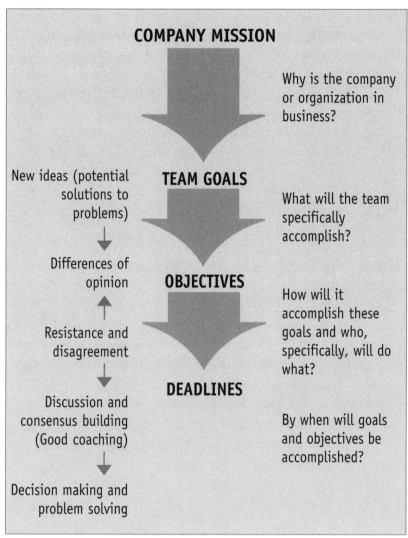

COMPANY MISSION

Why is the company or organization in business?

New ideas (potential solutions to problems)

TEAM GOALS

What will the team specifically accomplish?

Differences of opinion

OBJECTIVES

Resistance and disagreement

How will it accomplish these goals and who, specifically, will do what?

Discussion and consensus building (Good coaching)

DEADLINES

Decision making and problem solving

By when will goals and objectives be accomplished?

Fig. 3. *The strategic planning process.*

- **Follow through (norming).** Once a team has a strategic plan, it needs to take action! One big mistake a team can make is to develop a plan and then put it on the shelf in favor of doing the same old things the company has always done.

Have you ever been part of a group or team where everyone met frequently to discuss what they were going to do? There may have been much banter, but no commitment to action. Many of you have probably been part of this scenario at one time or another. Why do you suppose there was no commitment to action?

The primary reason that team members don't act or follow through is fear of risk or failure. The safe thing to do is to do nothing. In this case, the team becomes immobilized by its fears, and it's the team leader's job to keep the team moving forward.

In the follow-through stage, the team should monitor and measure its progress. If the goal is quantifiable, then the team should be able to know how it is performing. The role of the team leader is to coach and counsel team members as they are carrying out their goals and objectives. If team members are having difficulties, the team coach or leader should be assisting them or coaching them through the problems.

What if things are going well? Then the coach needs to provide plenty of recognition. One of the most important things the leader can do is give ongoing recognition for good performance. B.F. Skinner, one of the pioneers in organizational development referred to this as *random*

> "I always taught players that the main ingredient of stardom is the rest of the team. It's amazing how much can be accomplished if no one cares who gets the credit. That's why I was as concerned with a player's character as I was with his ability."
>
> —John Wooden (former coach, UCLA basketball team)

intermittent reinforcement. When people do good work, build their confidence. As employees grow in esteem and confidence, they take greater responsibility for their actions and make more of their own decisions. In other words, they mature as individuals and as a team. When that happens, they become more self-sufficient and less reliant on the team leader. They are then ready for the fourth and final stage of team development.

- **Transformation (performing).** At this stage, the team has been transformed from a group of individuals working together into a true team that exhibits many of the key traits discussed in Chapter 1: team members have become decision makers, problem solvers, conflict managers, and goal setters.

It means that the team is goal driven and that the team can be depended on to follow through consistently. The role of the team leader now becomes more of a counselor than a coach.

Who does most of the talking in a formal counseling session—the counselor or the patient? You probably answered, "the patient." Consider that analogy when thinking of the team leader's role in the transformation stage. Since the team is mature and performing effectively, the team leader needs to do more listening than talking. He or she becomes a "sounding board" for the team. Team members can share creative ideas, new concepts, and suggested goals with the team leader and ask for guidance. For the most part, however, the team is now making more of its own choices. Members are functioning as a self-directed team. Figure 4 shows the four stages of a team and the role of the team leader as the team progresses through the four stages.

"Kindness consists in loving people more than they deserve."

—Joseph Joubert

The Four Social Stages of Team Development

Team Stage	Team Coach's Roles	The Team Leader as Coach/ Counselor*	Level of Empower- ment
Defining (Focus on goal setting)	• Providing direction by suggesting goals • Orientation—explaining why certain goals could be important • Creating a "social comfort feel" by helping team members get to know each other • Setting a motivational climate	Coach	Low
Planning (Concentrate on strategic planning)	• Soliciting feedback about proposed goals • Encouraging participation and creativity • Coaching the discussion when there are differences • Managing conflict to reach agreement • Creating a climate of change • Helping to get resources	Coach/Counsel	Medium

* Coaching is a "directive process" where the coach does more speaking than listening.

Counseling is a "listening process" where the coach does more listening than talking.

Fig. 4. *The role of a team leader as a team passes through each stage of social development.*

The Four Social Stages of Team Development (Cont.)

Team Stage	Team Coach's Roles	The Team Leader as Coach/ Counselor*	Level of Empower-ment
Follow through (Take action toward goal achieving)	• Pushing people out of their comfort zones to take action • Monitoring action • Rewarding success as it happens • Assisting in correcting mistakes • Reviewing progress constantly	Counsel/Coach	High
Transformation (Mature as a team; team gets results and focuses on other goals)	• Delegating more decision making and problem solving to the team • Listening to team concerns • Suggesting alternatives to solve problems • Encouraging team members to solve their own problems	Counsel	Low
Celebration/ Evaluation**	• Recognizing team success • Celebrating with luncheon/ dinner meeting	Coach/Counsel	Medium

** This is not a state of development, but a conclusive behavior to bring closure to team goals so that team members realize the job is really done.

How Well Do You Coach and Counsel Your Team?

The team leader greatly influences a team's development. He or she creates a team climate of encouragement or discouragement. Rate yourself on a scale of 1 to 5 in regard to how well you perform each of these coaching and counseling functions. 1 is lowest, 5 is highest.

1. Define specifically suggested goals the team should be interested in   1   2   3   4   5

2. Give team members the opportunity to suggest their own goals and/or methods of accomplishing them   1   2   3   4   5

3. Coach the team to develop strategic plans for its goals   1   2   3   4   5

4. Encourage team members to present new ideas   1   2   3   4   5

5. Manage conflict/differences between and among team members   1   2   3   4   5

6. Build consensus and reach agreement   1   2   3   4   5

7. Encourage meaningful change, stand behind the change, and stay the course until the change is implemented   1   2   3   4   5

8. Get resources for team members to achieve success	1	2	3	4	5
9. Encourage sound risk taking	1	2	3	4	5
10. Encourage the team to take action on goals, decisions, and problem solving	1	2	3	4	5
11. Recognize good performance	1	2	3	4	5
12. Correct poor performance without condemning team members	1	2	3	4	5
13. Willing to take corrective action against team members who make the same mistakes over and over	1	2	3	4	5
14. Delegate as team members mature	1	2	3	4	5
15. Give feedback to team members on a continuing basis	1	2	3	4	5
16. Listen to team suggestions and concerns	1	2	3	4	5
17. Encourage mature teams to solve their own problems	1	2	3	4	5
18. Celebrate success	1	2	3	4	5

Add your totals and indicate your score:_____

- A score of 72 to 90 means you're providing a positive climate for your team to grow and mature.
- A score of 54 to 72 indicates a need to spend more time with your team to assist it through the four stages of team development.
- A score below 54 suggests that there are several areas of behavior you must concentrate on to help your team become mature and successful.

The Socialization of Teams: Understanding Their Social Needs

Teams need constant nurturing as they move through the social stages of development. Even when they have reached maturity, they need the support and guidance of the team leader and other managers and administrators. Here is a list of some of the needs your team members might have:

- *Technical skills training* to do their jobs effectively
- *Human relations skills training* such as conflict management, problem solving, communications, listening, and cultural diversity
- *The need for challenging work*—to conduct work above and beyond the routine
- *Resources*—time, budget, materials, and people
- *The opportunity for achievement*—to work in a climate that stresses achievement and success rather than failure and mistakes
- *Recognition*—to be recognized for their work
- *Belonging*—to be accepted by management and by each other
- *Fair pay* for the work being done
- *Incentives beyond regular pay*—bonuses, gifts, and discounts on products or services the company produces
- *To be listened to*—the team members' suggestions, ideas, problems, concerns, and fears need to be considered

"The measure of a man is not the number of his servants but in the number of people whom he serves."

—Dr. Paul D. Moody

- *To be empowered*—to empower team members to take responsibility for their own outcomes
- *To participate*—which goes hand in hand with empowerment
- *To be encouraged* rather than discouraged
- *To be informed*—to know what's going on in the organization
- *To be involved in making change*—not just be subjected to it

Striving for Continuous Improvement

Meeting team needs leads to yet another stage of team development—continuous improvement. Of course, this stage is meant to parallel the principles of Total Quality Management. Once again, TQM is the continuous improvement of goods, services, procedures, and people ultimately to serve customer needs more effectively.

In team building, then, it's important to assist the team that has reached the transformation stage so that team members and the team keep evolving.

The circle in figure 5 represents continuous improvement. Each time a team goal is accomplished, the team leader should help the team focus on a new challenge or goal.

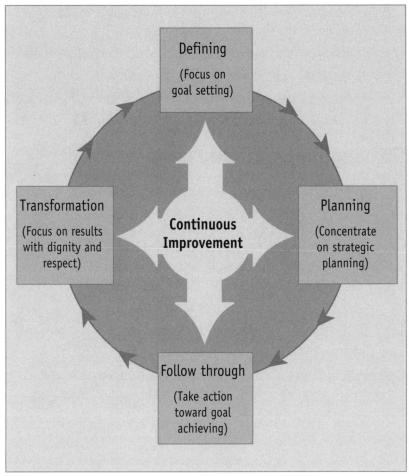

Fig. 5. *Circle of team development and continuous improvement.*

Defining Your Team's Stage of Development

Study the diagram on the next page to determine what stage of development your team is in presently. Place an X on the circular continuum at that stage. If you will be assessing more than one team, then photocopy this page and list the name of each team and rate it accordingly.

Another idea is to have individual team members rate where they think their team ranks in terms of its social development. Obviously for this exercise to work most effectively, it would be best to provide your team with some training about the stages of social development.

Notice the new terms that have been added in the diagram: infancy, childhood, adolescence, and maturity. Think of your team as a child growing into adulthood.

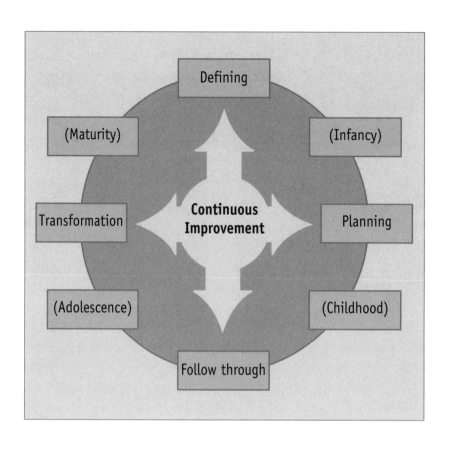

Defining Team Rules to Minimize Conflict

It's important to promote team harmony and to contain feuds and disagreements before they get out of hand. When a team is going through the various stages of development, there can be differences of opinion, differences in what team members value, and different ideas about what team rules should be.

One of the most important things a team should do in the defining stage of development is to define its own set of team rules or guidelines. If the team sets its own rules, then it determines its own standards for behavior. Team members become accountable to each other.

If the team leader sets the rules, then the team may choose not to take responsibility for living up to the rules. In fact, they may rebel against them.

The exercise on the next page is designed for your team to participate in. At your next team meeting, break the team into several groups and ask them to brainstorm a set of rules they will abide by. Then, bring the whole team together and have each group list its suggested rules. Have the team define which of the rules they all want to live with. These become the official team rules. Listed below is a step-by-step process your team can use to define its rules.

Step 1: Have a team meeting with the specific purpose of brainstorming a set of team rules.

Step 2: Explain to the team its task to set rules and the importance of the task. The rules become the set of behaviors team members are held accountable to follow.

Step 3: Ask the team to form groups to brainstorm the rules they would like to have. Ask each group to list their suggested rules on a flip chart.

Step 4: Have each group report its suggested rules to the overall team.

Step 5: From all these suggestions, ask the team to decide what rules they want to establish for the team as a whole.

"There is nothing so small that it can't be blown out of proportion."
—Ruchert's Law

Defining Rules Our Team Will Live By

Divide your team into groups that will make a list of suggested team rules. Be sure to list all suggestions. Later you can determine which of them the whole team wants to adopt and those the team doesn't want to commit to.

_____

_____

_____

_____

_____

_____

_____

_____

_____

_____

_____

_____

_____

_____

Below is a suggested list of team rules. Think of these only as suggestions to prompt your thinking. You may wish to add some of these to your list if your team feels comfortable with them.

- We will be on time, every time, in the delivery of our goods and services and for our team meetings.
- It's okay to disagree with each other, but it's not okay to be disagreeable.
- All team members will participate in problem solving and decision making.
- We will always strive for quality in producing goods and services.
- We will always strive to set goals that are measurable and attainable.
- If we disagree with each other, we will always make an honest attempt to resolve our differences.
- All team members will strive for open and honest communication.
- The team leader will coach team members to function effectively and efficiently.
- Regular training about technical skills and human relations will be a value to our team.
- Team members will take responsibility for their own outcomes.
- New team members will be welcomed to the team enthusiastically.
- We will be flexible and change-oriented rather than opposed to change.
- We will emphasize innovation and creativity.

3

Team
Building and
Personality
Style

Team Chemistry: Understanding Personality and Interpersonal Style Differences

Personality differences among team members have a profound impact on team development. Personalities, of course, are molded over time, and our basic values are formed, for the most part, in our childhood. When a group of people form a team, their personalities must learn to gel. This isn't always easy. Each of these individuals brings unique values and habits to the team. When team members discover these differences, they often begin to compete against each other or to attack one another. This is particularly true if the "team members" haven't been exposed to work teams before or if any team members grew up with the value of always playing to "win."

If team members, early in their team-building training, can be enlightened about personality differences, then they can understand *that people are very likely going to be different from each other.* What the team can learn is that there is nothing wrong with individual team members having different personalities. In fact, it can be a strength because each team member brings unique perspectives to the team, which enhances decision making and problem solving.

In the 1920s, the noted psychologist Carl Jung published research in which he concluded that there are four distinct personality styles and that each of us is composed of traits of all four styles. However, we all have one style that predominates, based on our values and habits.

"Each of us is worthy, not worthless; important, not insignificant; unique, not ordinary."

—William Arthur Ward

If you can be more aware of your personality style and the style of each of your team members, then you can understand what makes them behave the way they do and what they value. Here, your personality style refers to your interpersonal style in working with your team. If all team members can have greater awareness of each other, conflicts can be minimized and cooperation can more likely be attained.

On the following pages is an interpersonal style inventory called the *TEAM Interpersonal Style Evaluation*. First, photocopy it before you complete it so that later you can administer it to your whole team as a teaching exercise, keeping in mind these two points:

1. You can all benefit from learning more about your personality strengths.

2. It's helpful to know your fellow team members' personality strengths so that you can understand one another. Realize that just because you are different from each other doesn't mean you can't work together.

"We owe almost all of our knowledge not to those who have agreed but to those who differed."

—Charles Caleb Colton

TEAM Interpersonal Style Evaluation

This is an informal survey to help you understand and identify your unique interpersonal style in working with your team. It will focus on your strengths as an individual and also as a member of a team.

Read each set of statements below. In each pair, choose the one statement that describes you most when you're working with your team. Both statements may be true of you, but choose the one that applies to you in the most situations, most often, with the most people. Then, circle the letter in front of that statement.

1. D   I am often direct and frank in team meetings.

    C   I tend to be reserved and careful in team meetings.

2. D   I take control when there are crisis situations my team is confronted with.

    C   I tend to be more reflective and to see what happens before taking action when a crisis occurs.

3. B   My decision making with the team is usually based on intuition and feelings that I have or that are raised by team members.

    A   My decision making is usually based on facts, logic, and specific information I have or that is communicated by team members.

4. A   I tend not to express my emotions and feelings to team members.

    B   I often express my emotions and feelings to team members.

5. D I usually contribute information or add to team member discussions and team conversations.

   C I seldom contribute to team member discussions or team conversations since I prefer for them to solve their own problems.

6. C I am careful and contemplative about taking risks and accepting new, difficult challenges where the team could fail.

   D I am quick to take risks and accept new, difficult challenges even though some may be difficult for the team to accomplish.

7. B My facial expressions and enthusiasm in conveying my views or responding to the views of team members are greater than most people I know.

   A I tend to be less descriptive in my facial expressions and enthusiasm in conveying my views or in responding to the views of team members.

8. A I am usually a bit difficult to get to know in interpersonal situations and business situations.

   B I feel like I am easy to get to know both in interpersonal situations and in business situations.

9. C I usually make decisions deliberately, more slowly, and with forethought when I know my team will be affected.

   D I usually make my decisions quickly, spontaneously, and in the "heat of the moment."

10. B I am able to adapt to changing schedules and the whims of individuals around me.

    A I am more rigid and disciplined about how I spend my time.

11. D   I tend to use strong language and sometimes expressive gestures in communicating to team members, and I feel comfortable in stating my opinions.

     C   I tend not to raise my voice, use a harsh tone, or use dramatic gestures to express my views, feelings, and opinions to team members.

12. A   I emphasize planning and detailed information about who should do what, how it should be done, and when.

     B   I emphasize spontaneity and exciting and unplanned events that capture my attention.

13. B   My conversations with team members focus on personal experiences and other people in my life.

     A   My conversations with team members focus on my job, professional experiences, and the work of other people.

14. D   I tend to sometimes bend the rules to fit my needs and the team's needs.

     C   I always follow policies and rules in getting things done, and I encourage team members to do the same.

15. B   My body language and facial expressions tell people right away and with little doubt what I am thinking and feeling.

     A   My body language and facial expressions tend to be more reserved so as to disguise my true feelings and personal thoughts to team members.

16. B   I like to be out among my team members to get things done and to elicit their ideas.

     A   I prefer to work alone and to not be encumbered by the thoughts, ideas, and feelings of other team members.

17. D   I enjoy introducing myself to new team members and am willing to talk to them about myself and personal matters.

     C   I usually let new team members introduce themselves to me rather than approaching them first, and I am reluctant to get too personally involved.

18. D   In expressing myself and my views to the team, I often use dramatic statements such as "I think...," "I feel...," and "I believe that..."

     C   In expressing myself and my views to the team, I often use statements that defend and justify my beliefs such as, "According to others I have spoken to... ," "Based on a previous conversation...," and "Others have found that..."

Count how many times you have circled each letter:

A _____   B _____   C_____   D _____

(The combined total should equal 18.)

B minus A = _____

D minus C = _____

Continue to the next page for further instructions.

Analyzing the Results

To determine your personality type, plot your first score (B minus A) on the vertical scale and mark an X on the scale that represents your number. This number will be between -9 and +9.

Plot the second number (D minus C) on the horizontal scale. Place an X on the scale indicating your number, which will again be between -9 and +9. Now connect the two points by drawing a line out from each number until they intersect. The quadrant where the two points intersect indicates your TEAM interpersonal style:

T=Targeted

E=Enthusiastic

A=Accommodating

M=Meditative

The farther out you are in the quadrant, the more you exhibit that interpersonal style. The closer you are to the center and/or to another quadrant indicates that you still exhibit the characteristics of that interpersonal style but not as distinctly. If you are close to another quadrant, you have strong interpersonal strengths in both quadrants although the one you are in prevails.

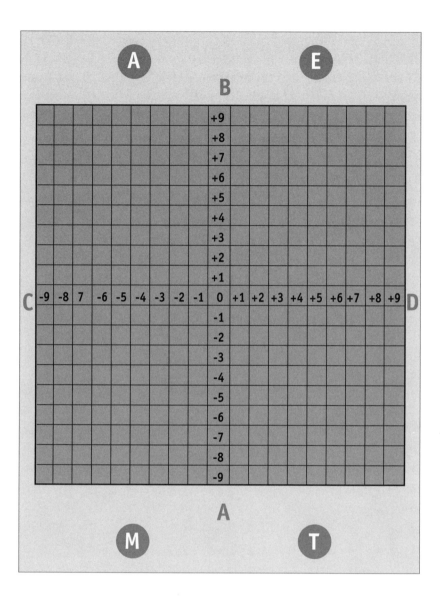

Take time to study the characteristics of each interpersonal style—they're presented in the quadrant on the next page. As you review the traits of the four interpersonal styles, think about your team. Is there diversity in interpersonal styles, or do you think that most team members have the same interpersonal style? When recruiting new members, does the team leader tend to recruit people who share his or her interpersonal style?

If all or most team members are of the same interpersonal style, the result will be "group think." As noted previously, when "group think" occurs, everyone tends to value the same behaviors and ideas. Thus, there may not be much creativity in goal setting, decision making, and problem solving.

When the team leader recruits people who are different from each other, there is diversity in behavior, opinions, and ideas. The team will likely be more creative in setting goals, make better decisions, and solve problems more effectively. Unfortunately, there may also be heightened conflict because the people on the team will disagree. The team leader must be effective at coaching and facilitating these different personalities to help them reach agreement.

Accommodating

- Focuses on team harmony and steadiness
- Creates a team climate of trust, dependability, and security
- Listens sincerely to team member feedback and ideas
- Tends to be more careful and contemplative with goals and actions the team should consider
- Tends to be indecisive under stress
- Open and considerate

Need: Personal assurance, comfort, direction, sincerity, slower methodical pace

Fear: Conflict

Enthusiastic

- Focuses on people and team member relationships
- Enjoys teamwork and people involvement
- Encourages team innovation
- Considers team member facts, opinions, and ideas
- Gets team members to do things by using persuasion more than power
- Tends to be impulsive under stress
- Optimistic

Need: Recognition, approval, fast pace, involvement, fun

Fear: Being disliked

Meditative

- Focuses on team analysis, facts, and detail
- Encourages the team to plan strategically and to focus on tasks
- Creates a climate where team rules are encouraged and followed
- Encourages the team to solve problems through effective analysis
- Doesn't encourage team spirit as much as team process
- Tends to withdraw under stress
- Contemplative and reserved

Need: To be right, slow pace for processing information, accuracy, time to be alone

Fear: Being wrong, quick change without substantiation

Targeted

- Focuses on team goals and results
- Expects team to take action and be decisive
- Encourages risk taking
- Expresses own opinions and feelings freely to the team
- Doesn't encourage a lot of interpersonal team member involvement
- Tends to be controlling when under stress
- Competitive

Need: Control, fast pace, independence, accomplishment

Fear: Being taken advantage of

Understanding, Diversity, and Tolerance

Keep in mind that your team's diversity can be its strength.

Diversity is an intrinsic part of the Earth and its people. There are differences in nature and in species.

Think about a world made up of just one kind of animal or flower or tree. What if there was only one season and one reason to do something of value?

What if there was just one color of people or one religion for everyone? And, if there was only one point of view, there would be no reason for striving.

Yet with diversity comes disagreement, pain, and sometimes sorrow. For the human spirit is fragile and delicate, yet contentious.

This contradiction in behavior causes us to sometimes embrace diverse opinions and peoples, and, at other times, without proper reasoning, may force contempt, fear, and loathing.

What we don't know we often fear; who we don't know sometimes causes suspicion and close-mindedness, preventing progress.

Welcome and hold diversity dear. To be open to the values of others, the differences in people and things is to more likely secure a positive future.

To rise above sameness and the ordinary shows strength of character, confidence, and richness in opportunity.

So,

Seek and *praise* the uniqueness of others.

Be willing to *listen* with an open mind.

Embrace those ideas you hold in esteem.

Remain open to those ideas and people whose values are different than yours.

Be *just* yet *gentle* in stating your views.

Preserve the delicacy of the human spirit.

Love all things in nature and its people, for loving ensures abundance in life.

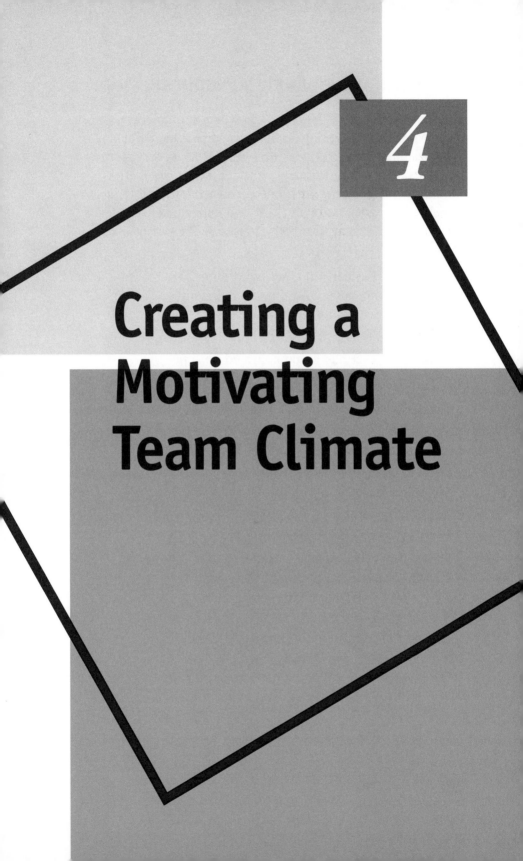

4

Creating a Motivating Team Climate

Motivation: Everybody's Responsibility

For teams to succeed, the climate in which team members work must be positive, inspiring, and motivational. One definition of organizational climate is *what an employee feels and experiences once he or she works in your organization and becomes acquainted with its culture and the leadership style.* If the team member likes what he or she feels and experiences, that team member is apt to stay. If not, the person is likely to move on.

Some employees actually leave. Others stay in the organization and move on mentally. In other words, they lose motivation for their job. As you can see, setting the right kind of climate for team members is critical to team success. Consider these two questions:

1. Have you ever met an unmotivated person?

2. Can you motivate other people?

Chances are you answered the first question with a "yes." Most people would indeed claim to personally know unmotivated people. In fact, you could be working next to one each day.

I met a stranger in the night whose lamp had ceased to shine,
and I paused to let him light his light from mine;
A tempest sprang up later on and shook the world about,
and when the wind was gone my lamp was out;
But back to me the stranger came
his lamp was glowing fine,
He held the precious flame, and lighted mine.

—Author Unknown

But stop to consider this: What happens to these unmotivated people about five o'clock in the afternoon, or whenever they get off work? They get motivated! Right?

Chances are you too get motivated at five o'clock to get off work and go home to your family and hobbies and other important aspects of your life. So, you see, everyone is motivated. The secret is finding out what motivates each person. As a team leader, one of your challenges is dealing with team members who aren't motivated at work. Why aren't they motivated? Try the following exercise to get at the crux of that question.

"The price of greatness is responsibility."

—Winston Churchill

Determining the Causes of a Lack of Motivation

List here the reasons why employees may not be motivated. Then compare your answers to the list on the next page.

_____

_____

_____

_____

_____

_____

_____

_____

_____

_____

_____

_____

_____

_____

_____

_____

_____

_____

Here is a list of some of the reasons why team members may not be motivated to do good work:

- Lack of challenging work
- Lack of opportunity for achievement, including lack of resources
- Little or no recognition for work that's done
- Lack of belonging, or isolation from the team
- Work that provides no real sense of purpose
- Personal problems
- Work ethic is not valued
- Poor communication
- Unclear goals, or none at all
- No empowerment
- Creativity and open communication is discouraged
- Team members threatened for making mistakes

Again consider the question: Have you ever met an unmotivated person? If you look at all the reasons why team members may be unmotivated, you'll see that most of them relate to the organizational climate. Often the leader can influence the organizational climate.

As you should be able to see by now, the answer to the question "Have you ever met an unmotivated person?" is an emphatic "no." There is no such thing. Everyone is motivated to do *something*. Unfortunately, some people are just motivated to go home, in part, because they work in an unmotivating climate.

Whose role is it to create a motivating climate so the team can be successful? The *team leader's.* He or she is responsible for creating opportunities for achievement by providing resources, assisting team members in goal setting, giving recognition for good performance, helping team members feel like they belong, and communicating effectively.

Now let's address the second question: Can you motivate other people? The answer again is an emphatic "no." People must be self-motivated.

Managers and team leaders sometimes go out of their way to try to motivate people who choose not to be motivated. They spend a great deal of time and effort trying to get these unmotivated people to change, and they do it at the expense of team members who deserve the leader's time and positive recognition.

To summarize these two key points, remember:

1. The team leader is responsible for creating a motivating climate.

2. The team members are *personally* responsible for acting and following through in such a climate.

Accepting Personal Responsibility

One of the most important traits of effective team members is *responsibility*. When organizations move from a traditional hierarchy to a team-building structure, three important things should happen:

1. Team leaders or supervisors should share power with team members to set goals, make decisions, and solve problems.

2. Team members should assume responsibility to take charge and hold themselves accountable for the outcomes related to their goals, decisions, and solutions to their problems.

3. The team leader should support team members' actions and efforts, providing praise when they succeed and coaching them through their mistakes.

Team building is a growth process. It's unrealistic to expect team members to assume a great deal of responsibility in the early stages of team building if they have traditionally always been told what to do. The transfer of power and responsibility needs to be gradual. In fact, if it's thrust on team members all at once, particularly those accustomed to working under autocratic managers, the result is likely to be *a lack of motivation.*

For years, employees have been asking to have more responsibility for their own outcomes and for a long time management said: "No, we know what's best for you. Do what we tell you to do."

Then Total Quality Management and team building became popular and supervisors began to say: "Okay, maybe you're right. We want you to set goals, make decisions, and solve problems."

Employees said, "We're only joking."

What were they really saying? Chances are what they were thinking, is this: If we make mistakes, what will happen to us?

If team members make mistakes, the team leader should coach them instead of "flogging" them. Yes, personal responsibility is essential to a well-functioning, motivated team. But if team members live in fear of being chastised every time they make the wrong decision, they'll quickly learn to be motivated only to make "safe" decisions that continue the status quo. Growth stagnates and progress stalls.

"Loved people are loving people."

—Ann Landers

Management's Assumptions About Motivating Employees

Sometimes it's difficult for management to understand what motivates team members. Here are some reasons why:

1. Different team members are motivated by different things.

2. Team members don't always state directly what they want.

3. Team members sometimes don't know what they want.

4. Managers make assumptions about what motivates employees.

If the team leader (management) makes too many assumptions about what motivates employees, a great deal of time and effort can be wasted. Fortunately, through the years, employees have been asked to identify what motivates them. The list of motivators hasn't changed very much over time. Managers have also been asked to identify what they think motivates employees. Complete the exercise on the next page to find out whether your ideas about motivation match up with what team members think.

Forget their mistakes and zero in on one small thing they do right. Praise them and they'll do more things right and discover talents and abilities they never realized they had."

—Mary Kay Ash, founder of Mary Kay Cosmetics

Identifying and Ranking Motivators

Read the following list of motivators. Rank how you think employees rated these motivators and then how you feel managers ranked the motivators. A "1" is the highest ranking; a "10" is the lowest.

	Employee Ranking	Management Ranking
Feeling of being in on things (participation)		
Full appreciation of work completed		
Good working conditions		
Help on personal problems (empathy)		
High wages		
Interesting work		
Job security		
Personal loyalty of supervisor		
Promotion in the company		
Tactful discipline		

Now, compare your rankings with the actual rankings, based on research, listed on the next page.

	Employee Average	Management Average
Feeling of being in on things (participation)	2	10
Full appreciation of work completed	1	8
Good working conditions	9	4
Help on personal problems (empathy)	3	9
High wages	5	1
Interesting work	6	5
Job security	4	2
Personal loyalty of supervisor	8	6
Promotion in the company	7	3
Tactful discipline	10	7

How well did your answers compare? Note that what the employees ranked as 1, 2, and 3 the managers ranked as 8, 10, and 9. Employees say they want appreciation, to participate, and empathy and understanding. What do managers think workers want? Money, job security, and promotion.

Managers often assume that if you give employees money they will be motivated. Why do they think this? In part, because employees have told them so. They ask for more money thinking they will be motivated. Unfortunately, two weeks after receiving a raise, they may well feel unmotivated if they don't get any

"I can live for two months on a good compliment."

—Mark Twain

recognition (appreciation); if they don't get to participate in goal setting, problem solving, and decision making; and if managers don't listen to their concerns.

Although money does motivate some employees, research shows that most are driven more by intrinsic factors. This research is important because it provides you with a foundation for what motivates your team. But every team is different, so you'll have to determine what motivates your particular team members. Here are two critical techniques:

1. Observation

2. Listening for their needs (Remember, they don't always say directly what they want, and different people want different things.)

One of the big mistakes a team leader can make is to assume that what drives him or her will also motivate team members. Remember, we're all different. Consider the following Chinese folktale:

> A seagull got lost in flight. He thought he was flying towards the ocean, but was actually flying inland. He flew and flew and became very tired. Nearly spent, he looked around for a place to land.

> In the distance, the seagull saw the palace wall of a great king. Almost exhausted, he made his way to the wall and landed on it. The king saw the seagull sitting on the wall breathing deeply.

> The king had never before seen a seagull. He had only been told about them and what they looked like. He said to himself that this must be a great feat for a seagull to fly this far inland.

> The king decided that the seagull should be honored. He invited him into the castle. The king then invited the townspeople and the farmers from all around to the castle for a great celebration to honor the seagull.

They feasted on meat and wine. One day turned into two and the second day into three. As the hours and days went by, the seagull grew weaker and weaker and finally died, for the seagull did not like to eat meat or drink wine.

The moral of the story is that the king treated the seagull the way a king likes to be treated instead of treating the seagull the way a seagull likes to be treated.

Keep this story in mind as you consider what motivates your team members. You may be motivated by challenge or money or intrigue. But your team members may be motivated by something else.

Remember:

You can't motivate people, but you can create a climate where people *choose* to be motivated!

Exercise:

Defining the Climate in Your Organization

How's the weather in your organization? Do you create a motivational climate where team members want to stay, grow, and prosper? Is it sunny and bright, or is it cloudy and rainy?

Answer the questions below by circling the number that best describes the degree to which you accomplish the stated behavior or task. A "1" indicates areas where improvement is needed. A "5" means you do an excellent job.

1. Do you provide team members with challenging work? 1 2 3 4 5

2. Do you give team members authority and responsibility to solve problems and make decisions? 1 2 3 4 5

3. Do you reward people for achievement? 1 2 3 4 5

4. Do you strive for an atmosphere of trust? 1 2 3 4 5

5. Do you provide team members with a sense of direction? That is, do you assist them in defining goals and strategies? 1 2 3 4 5

6. Do you make team members feel like they belong? 1 2 3 4 5

7. Do you emphasize innovation and creativity?

    1   2   3   4   5

8. Do you encourage flexibility, risk taking, and change?

    1   2   3   4   5

Scoring:

Add the circled numbers to get a total, which is your final score.

Total Score _____

If you scored between 30 and 40, you're under the influence of a "high pressure system." Your organization is experiencing sunny and fair weather with a warm temperature. There's probably warmth, excitement, and enthusiasm among team members.

A score of 13 to 29 indicates a partly cloudy and mild climate. There may be some instability, but if you have a strong umbrella (good structure and good insulation), you can weather the storm.

If you scored from 1 to 12, your organization may be experiencing "low pressure." You may be on the brink of a storm with powerful wind and rain.

Now let your team members participate in this same exercise, reproduced on the next page. The questions have been changed to reflect their perspective. Photocopy the exercise and encourage each team member to complete it anonymously. Have one trusted team member collect all the completed instruments and tally the results. Then figure the average score for each of the questions to see how your team perceives the organizational climate.

Team Climate Survey

Answer the questions below by circling the number that best describes the degree to which you think your team accomplishes the stated behavior or task. A "1" indicates areas where improvement is needed. A "5" means you do an excellent job.

1. Is the work you carry out on your team, for the most part, challenging? 　　1　2　3　4　5

2. Do you feel like you are given reasonable authority and responsibility to solve problems and make decisions? 　　1　2　3　4　5

3. Do you feel you are recognized for your achievements? 　　1　2　3　4　5

4. Is there an atmosphere of trust on the team? 　　1　2　3　4　5

5. Are the team goals and strategies clear? 　　1　2　3　4　5

6. Do you feel as though you really belong (are you accepted as a team member)? 　　1　2　3　4　5

7. Are you encouraged to be innovative and creative? 　　1　2　3　4　5

8. Do you feel that risk taking and change are encouraged? 　　1　2　3　4　5

Scoring:

Add the circled numbers to give you a total.

Total Score _____

30 to 40: "High pressure system" climate—sunny, warm, and fair weather.

13 to 29: "Partly cloudy and mild"—some instability but you and your team strive to weather the storm.

1 to 12: "Low pressure system"—you may be on the brink of a storm.

Remember, as the team leader, you determine the climate. Here is your opportunity to control the weather on your team. First, answer the following questions, basing your responses on the results of your own organizational weather analysis and on the results of the Team Climate Survey. Then make a contract with yourself or someone else in the organization to change the weather for the better!

1. What are my strengths in creating a positive organizational climate? _____

   _____

   _____

   _____

   _____

   _____

   _____

   _____

   _____

2. What are my weaknesses that are keeping me from creating a positive team climate? _____

_____

_____

_____

_____

_____

_____

_____

_____

_____

3. As a result of this climate analysis, how will I change my behavior? _____

_____

_____

_____

_____

_____

_____

_____

_____

_____

_____

YOU CAN HAVE AN IMPACT ON THE WEATHER!

5

Building Trust

The Myth of Trust

Do team members automatically trust each other? The obvious answer is no. Often, team members don't trust each other or the team leader, and sometimes team leaders don't trust the team members.

But some managers automatically assume that people they place on teams will work together in harmony, that they'll cooperate with each other and get along wonderfully. This is an unrealistic expectation. Remember that teams go through stages before members gel and begin working toward a focused goal (see Chapter 2).

One of the signs of a team in the transformation stage is that team members trust each other. Take a few minutes to jot down some of the behaviors that the team leader and team members must model for trust to develop. Then compare you answers to the ideas discussed in this chapter.

> "Watch your thoughts; they become words.
>
> Watch your words; they become actions.
>
> Watch your actions; they become habits.
>
> Watch your habits; they become character.
>
> Watch your character; it becomes your destiny."
>
> —Frank Outlaw

Team Leader	Team Members
_____	_____
_____	_____
_____	_____
_____	_____
_____	_____
_____	_____

What You Can Do to Build Trust

Whether you're a team leader or a team member, it's important that you consistently model the behaviors that build trust among team members. Here are some of the essential behaviors that are important to model:

- **Always follow through on your commitments and values.** For team members to trust each other, they must consistently do what they say they will do. And if you're a team leader, you should live up to your obligations with team members and follow through on what you say you value. For instance, if you say you value team members showing up on time for meetings, then you must show up on time.

- **Always meet deadlines.** Trust builds when people perform their responsibilities and meet their goals on time. Always live up to deadlines you commit to. If something beyond your control happens that will keep you from meeting a deadline, then quickly inform others who are affected.

"The only way to make a man trustworthy is to trust him."

—Henry L. Stimson

- **Trust others.** Trust begets trust. If you want others to trust you, then trust them unless they give you good reason not to. What if someone betrays your trust? First, try to find out why. Second, put your future expectations with such team members in writing.

- **Self-disclose.** Share knowledge with team members. Give them any information you can that will help them be successful. If others see that you're trying to be helpful, they'll be more likely to share information and knowledge. Withholding knowledge sends the message that you want to "win." Self-disclosure says you want team members to be empowered.

- **Empower team members.** Empowering others shows that you trust them. Demonstrate your trust by allowing and encouraging team members to make decisions and solve problems.

- **Resolve conflicts early.** Show your desire to get beyond disagreement. Conflict escalates because it appeals to people's competitive nature. Show your willingness to cooperate rather than compete by striving for win-win solutions to differences and problems.

"A true friend never gets in your way unless you happen to be going down."

—Arnold H. Glasow

- **Respect the differences in people.** As discussed in Chapter 2, people have different personalities, values, skills, and backgrounds. Show your willingness to accept people who are different from you.

- **Demonstrate personal integrity.** Be professional in your relationships. Live by a moral code. One definition of a professional is this: "a person who has been certified either by degree or special testing to have specific knowledge and skill in some discipline and who demonstrates a moral obligation to use the skills and knowledge with integrity." An accountant, an engineer, or a plumber can be called a professional. However, if that person does not have integrity in the eyes of customers or constituents, then he or she really isn't.

- **Be honest.** In a study that asked employees to identify what they perceived to be the most important traits of leadership, *honesty* was rated the highest, with 87 percent of all participants listing it as the most important. (*Source:* "The Credibility Factor: What Followers Expect From Their Leaders." James M. Kouzes and Barry Z. Posner. *Management Review,* Jan. 1990. pp. 29-33.)

"I'd much rather deal with someone who's good at their job but malevolent toward me, than someone who likes me but is a ninny."

—Sam Donaldson

An easy way to remember the basic behaviors for building trust is this acronym: RELIABLE. You may want to take the information from this page, enlarge it on a copy machine, put it on a piece of cardboard, and hang it in the room where you hold most of your team meetings:

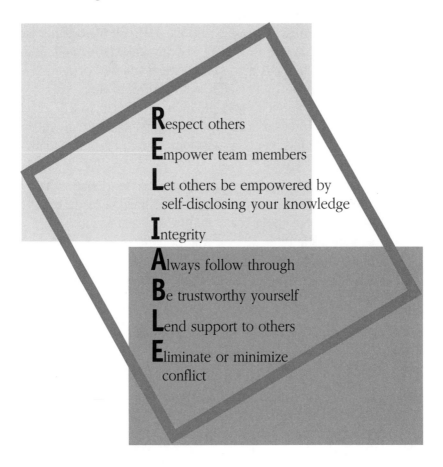

Respect others

Empower team members

Let others be empowered by
  self-disclosing your knowledge

Integrity

Always follow through

Be trustworthy yourself

Lend support to others

Eliminate or minimize
  conflict

"No person was ever honored for what he received. Honor has been the reward for what he gave."

—Calvin Coolidge

Using the Johari Window to Build Trust and Openness

More than twenty years ago, Joseph Luft and Harry Ingham developed a grid to describe the dynamics of communications and trust (see fig. 6). Called the "Johari Window," after the two psychologists who developed it—Joe and Harry—it serves as an excellent model for discussing how team members and the team leader must disclose information to each other to build the trust that's necessary for effectively solving problems and making decisions.

	Known to Self	Unknown to Self
Known to Others	Public	Blind
Unknown to Others	Hidden	Unknown

Fig. 6. *Johari Window*

The window tracks information that can influence a situation. The *public* square contains information known to both or all parties. The *blind* square shows what others know that you don't. The *hidden* square contains information that you know but others don't. The *unknown* square contains what you and the other team members are blind to or that neither of you know. It is information that still needs to be discovered.

Moving Beyond Hidden Agendas and Distrust

Scenario #1: First Encounters (when teams form)

Public	Blind
Hidden	Unknown

When team members and the team leader first meet one another, the unknown window is dominant. But if the team leader begins self-disclosing (e.g., identifying an agenda for the team, setting team goals, providing background information), in other words, modeling "open behavior," team members will feel encouraged to do the same. Sharing of information establishes an atmosphere of cooperation. If team members don't start out cooperating with each other, they will compete with each other (see scenario #2). As a team leader, strive to help your team achieve the climate in scenario #3.

"Loved people are loving people."

—Ann Landers

Scenario #2: Hidden Agendas (when team members distrust each other)

Public	Blind
Hidden	Unknown

Here, each team member develops a hidden agenda to which other team members are blind. And why not? Since people in our culture often grow up competing against each other, they see that withholding information and knowledge gives them a competitive advantage. A team leader is vital at this point. A team leader who wants to compete against team members won't share information and knowledge. Instead of empowering others, the team leader uses power over them. This, of course, encourages team members to do the same thing. Such a climate becomes very destructive because team members are always devising ways to "get each other." Rather than cooperation, there is derision, hostility, and dissension. Eventually, the team may self-destruct.

> *"You can buy people's time; you can buy their presence at a given place; you can even buy a measured number of their skilled muscular motions per hour. But you cannot buy enthusiasm ... you cannot buy loyalty ... you cannot buy the devotion of hearts, minds, or souls. You must earn these.*
>
> —Clarence Francis

Scenario #3: Shared Information (empowerment and trust)

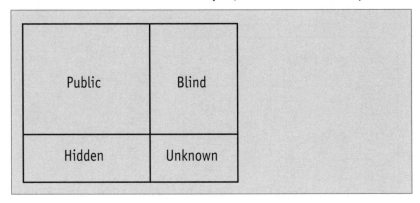

Scenario #1 describes the climate that dominates when team members first meet each other. For trust to develop, the team leader must set the example. By sharing information, opening the "public" window, the leader creates an environment in which open communication can take place.

Remember the four stages of team development? The first stage is "defining." The leader can plant the seeds of open communication by defining: by providing direction and sharing information about expectations, team goals, and responsibilities. If the team leader models self-disclosure, then team members will more likely do the same. Once team members are comfortable doing so, they can set goals, solve problems, and make decisions together.

Knowing When to Go Public

Scenario #1	Scenario #2	Scenario #3

Public	Blind
Hidden	Unknown

Public	Blind
Hidden	Unknown

Public	Blind
Hidden	Unknown

The spirit of the "Johari Window" as it relates to team building is that self-disclosure empowers people and helps them to set goals, solve problems, and make decisions cooperatively. For teams to be successful, this kind of spirit is essential.

However, common sense dictates that the team leader can't share all information with team members (e.g., salary information), nor do most team members feel comfortable sharing their innermost thoughts with everyone on the team.

The truth is that everyone has "hidden" information, information they won't share, for whatever reason. And everyone has a "blind spot," information they don't know about others. And there will always be "unknown information," that which team members haven't yet discovered.

As a team leader, if you can create a climate of self-disclosure and trust, team members will be more willing to shrink the "unknown." If a spirit of creativity exists, team members will focus on discovering and sharing possible new (previously unknown) solutions to problems. This style of cooperation enhances decision making and yields greater productivity.

The bottom line is this: Strive to encourage disclosure and sharing because it creates trust, but respect each person's privacy.

Coach/
Counselor/
Facilitator:
The Changing
Role of the
Team Leader

Leaders Are Made, Not Born

Leadership is the ability to help your team define what is important to accomplish (*goals* and priorities); to get *results* through *coaching, counseling,* and *resources;* and to help the team members *grow* in the process.

There are some important words in the above definition:

1. **Goals.** Leadership is about "rising above the minutiae" or the ordinary. It is helping team members decide what is important to accomplish.

2. **Results.** The leader's role is to remove obstacles so that team members can successfully accomplish goals and other important work. Too often, however, "leaders" create obstacles such as too much bureaucracy, too many reports, lack of feedback, lack of direction, and putdowns. Real leaders "clear the path" to success and guide team members toward achievement.

3. **Coaching and counseling.** To coach is to provide direction. To counsel is to facilitate and assist team members in goal setting, decision making, and problem solving. The difference between these two leadership roles will become clear as you read this chapter.

4. **Resources.** Leaders must provide resources—time, money, people, materials, and equipment—for team members to accomplish goals and priorities.

"We may give advice, but we cannot inspire the conduct."

—François de La Rochefoucauld, French politician and writer

Consider this example:

The coach of a professional football team asks the players at the beginning of the year: "What's our goal this year?"

The likely answer is, "To win the Super Bowl."

But what if the team coach then says: "Well, that's a good goal. However, I just had a discussion with upper management and they said we must cut back on our resources to save money, so I'm going to have to ask all of you to play without helmets and pads this year."

Pretty silly, right? But people in business and industry are being asked, figuratively speaking, to play without helmets and pads everyday. And they're getting beaten up and bloodied. Real leaders help team members get the resources they need.

5. **Growth.** Part of leadership is helping others to learn through training, guidance and direction, and personal experience. It's not enough just to get results. Those who attain the results must be transformed into something more than they were previously. A real leader wants to see team members prosper. Leaders aren't afraid to see team members grow for fear that their own positions will be threatened. Real leaders are empowering. "Supposed leaders" are overpowering—they have an attitude of "I'll tell you what I think you need to know, but nothing more."

"The person I work for is everything you could ever want in an ex-boss."

—Current Comedy

Differences Among Management and Leadership Styles

The style of management that has traditionally been modeled in most companies and organizations is *autocratic.* This style of management is characterized by an "us versus them" mentality. This "what I say goes" style pits managers and workers against each other.

New managers and team leaders tend to model what they have learned when they assume a position of authority. If they mostly learned to be autocratic, that is the management style they will use, particularly under pressure.

As you can probably guess, however, employees and team members are most likely to respond more positively to a democratic management style. People generally want to participate in their own goal setting, decision making, and problem solving. And remember from Chapter 5 that employees who are involved are more likely to be motivated. If this is true, then why do some managers and team leaders continue to use an autocratic management style? Here are several reasons:

1. It's always been used; therefore, it must work.

2. It's easy and doesn't require much time.

3. The "leader" feels in control.

4. The "leader" maintains power.

5. It creates "fear motivation," which appears to work—in the short run anyway.

6. Some supervisors have low self-esteem. Wielding power puts them in control psychologically.

Too often team leaders feel they must assert themselves to show that they are in control, so they bark out orders, define methods to accomplish work, set ambiguous deadlines (get this done as soon as possible), and "beat people up" mentally when they start making mistakes.

But these leaders aren't really being assertive. They're being aggressive—and there's a big difference between the two. In the context discussed here, to be *aggressive* is to compete against team members, either inadvertently or intentionally.

To be *assertive* is to provide direction to team members and to build relationships. When team members make mistakes, assertive behavior is to coach members through them.

Figure 7 shows the gradual change in the leadership role of the team leader as a team progresses through the four social stages of team development discussed in Chapter 2.

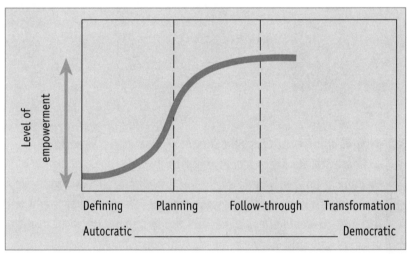

Fig. 7. *Role of leader at various stages of team development.*

Note that in the early stages of team development, when team leaders are new to the team or the team members are new to the team leader and each other, it is important for the leader to be assertive and direct. Team members need to know where the leader stands. The team leader must clearly state early on some of the potential goals, priorities, and tasks the team should work on as well as some of his or her beliefs and values, although not with the idea of forcing them on team members. To a degree, then, team leaders must be autocratic in the early stages of team development. But, as the team matures and builds trust by following through with its responsibilities, the team leader can become more democratic.

> General and former President Dwight D. Eisenhower used to demonstrate the art of leadership with a simple piece of string. He'd put it on a table and say: "Pull it and it'll follow wherever you wish. Push it and it will go nowhere at all." It's just that way when it comes to leading people. Leadership isn't something that comes automatically just because you have people working for you. Leadership depends on followers. If people don't follow a manager's lead voluntarily, if they always have to be forced, that person is not a good leader.
>
> Source: Bits & Pieces, Vol. N/No. 3. p. 4, 1991.

Conveying Expectations and Beliefs to Team Members

While it isn't a good idea as a team leader to force your values on other people, it is helpful to convey what you value so team members know where you stand. They won't all agree with you, but if you consistently model your beliefs, they will likely respect you for who you are and what you stand for.

The following list contains several values that you may wish to impart. Read through them, and check those that are important to you. Add any that aren't listed as well.

☐ On-time performance   ☐ Decision-making ability

☐ Courteousness and friendliness   ☐ Fairness

☐ Personal responsibility   ☐ Being goal-oriented

☐ Recognizing the accomplishments of others   ☐ Accessibility

☐ Humor

☐ Succinct communications   ☐ Hard work

☐ Effective listening   ☐ Effective time

☐ Giving regular feedback   ☐ Professionalism

☐ Honesty and truthfulness   ☐ Empowering others

☐ Understanding and empathy   ☐ Integrity

☐ Getting along with others

☐ Others _____   ☐ _____

☐ _____   ☐ _____

☐ _____   ☐ _____

☐ _____   ☐ _____

☐ _____   ☐ _____

Figure 7 illustrated how the team leader's role changes as the relationship between the leader and the team develops. As team members become more mature in working with each other, accomplishing goals and tasks, solving problems, and making decisions, the leader's role shifts from autocratic to democratic.

Chapter 1 illustrated the various types of teams and the leadership role of the "team coach." Figure 8 illustrates the same concept.

Figure 9 shows how the team leader role should change as the team begins to mature and as trust develops not only between the leader and team members but also among team members themselves.

Notice that the Telling style of leadership indicates that the leader simply tells team members what to do, how to do it, and when. It is the "my way or the highway" mentality. Certainly, in some instances, the team leader must be very assertive, particularly

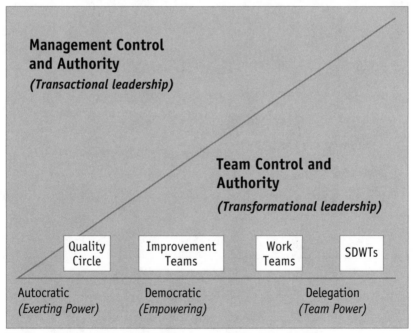

Fig. 8. *Role of the team leader for various types of teams.*

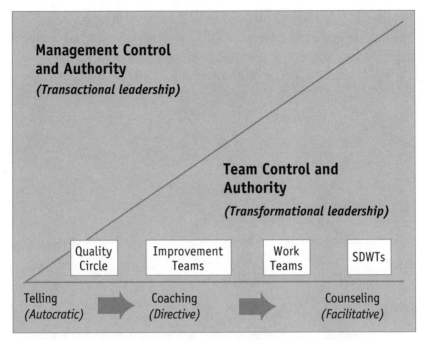

Fig. 9. *Changing role of team leader as team develops.*

when the team is new and needs considerable direction. Note that a quality circle falls between telling and coaching because members of a quality circle need considerable direction.

A team leader should assume a coaching role early in the team-building process. In this role, the leader shares authority with team members. The team leader's behavior is empowering. The idea is to get team members to be more involved in their own outcomes. However, since the team is still maturing, the team leader needs to guide or direct the process.

> *"There is nothing more difficult to take in hand, more perilous to conduct, or more uncertain in its success than to take the lead in the introduction of a new order of things."*
>
> *—Niccolo Machiavelli,* The Prince

When a team has demonstrated its ability to set and follow through on goals, to solve problems, and to make decisions, the team leader can assume a "counseling role," as illustrated in figure 9. Here, the leader is in a facilitative role, doing more listening than directing. He or she becomes a sounding board for the team. The team can begin to move toward self-direction.

Exercise:

Mark an X on the continuum below to describe the leadership style you use most of the time. What are the reasons you are using this style?

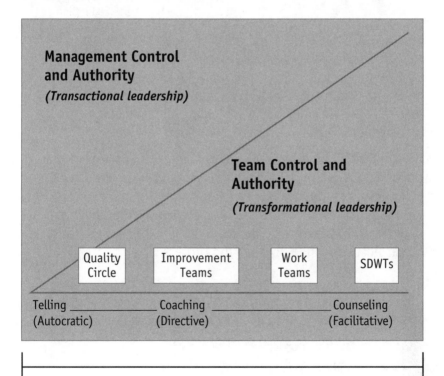

Management Control and Authority
(Transactional leadership)

Team Control and Authority
(Transformational leadership)

| Quality Circle | Improvement Teams | Work Teams | SDWTs |

| Telling | Coaching | Counseling |
| (Autocratic) | (Directive) | (Facilitative) |

Raising children parallels helping teams to mature

When children are very young, you must tell them what to do, how to do it and when. You are more autocratic and tell them to brush their teeth, not to go in the street, or to mind their manners.

As they get older and can reason for themselves, it's important to encourage them to make more of their own choices, to empower them to make decisions. Then as they make life choices, you encourage them, praising them when they do well and coaching them through their mistakes.

If you have empowered them as young children, then when they reach their teen years, they're used to making their own choices and are likely to have greater self-esteem. Through their teen years, as you continue to empower them, they will mature and become self-directed.

When they become adults and are on their own, they are apt to seek your advice. What they really want is for you to listen and to counsel them, although they are capable of making their own choices.

Here are some practical reminders for moving through the coaching/counseling continuum:

1. **Remember that improvement teams and work teams aren't always permanent.** They may exist to improve a process, to design or change a product or service, or to solve a problem; therefore, they may not and probably won't mature to a self-directed state. Leaders of such teams should strive for a shared decision-making role, one of coach/counselor. In other words, as the team is striving to accomplish its goal, there will be times when the leader should provide considerable direction. At other times, it will be more important to counsel team members to make their own decisions and to facilitate the process. The leader will need to judge which role is most effective at which times.

2. **Don't expect permanent teams to mature overnight.** As discussed previously, it takes time for trust to develop and for team members to learn to cooperate rather than to compete against each other. A department of people that becomes a team must assume greater responsibility for decision making and problem solving. If workers have been used to just "coming in and doing their work," it will take time for them to get used to taking charge. The team leader shouldn't try to rush the empowerment process. A team must be able to move through the development stages and mature over time. As it does so, the team leader's role gradually shifts from coach to counselor.

3. **Team leaders need training.** They need to know that building a mature team is a process of "group dynamics." Leaders need to understand the differences in people, their competitive nature, how to "direct" conflict, how to assist in problem solving and decision making, how to assist teams with goal setting and strategic planning and how to give team members effective feedback.

4. **Team leaders need to spend more time listening and less time talking as the team moves through the stages of development.** In a formal patient/counselor relationship, who does more talking, the patient or the counselor? The patient. The counselor asks more questions, trying to assist the patient in making his or her own choices through guidance. Counselors are often called "guidance" counselors. Encourage your "patients" to do more talking and decision making (see fig. 10).

"The art and science of asking questions is the source of all knowledge."

—Dr. Adolf Berle

Fig. 10. *Team leaders do more talking in the early stages of team development; more listening in the later stages.*

5. **The team leader should not use the coaching/counseling role as a way to manipulate team members.** If the team leader uses the coaching/counseling role as a guise to use power over people, then the leader is still an autocrat under a new label: coach. If the leader gives team members more responsibility, they must also have authority, or be empowered to carry out those responsibilities. Again, the transition to greater empowerment should be gradual (see fig. 11).

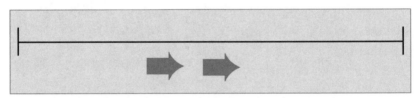

Fig. 11. *Team leader gradually releases more authority to team members in later stages of team development.*

6. **A final reminder: Always recognize team members for their efforts and successes.** If you want team members to change behaviors—to become more team-oriented and responsible—then it is important to reward those behaviors. Remember, you get what you reward, so reward behaviors that are team-oriented.

"In simplest terms, a leader is one who knows where he wants to go, and gets up and goes."

—John Erskine

Leadership Proficiency Profile

Rate yourself on some of the key characteristics of leaders, based on numerous studies of what comprises leadership. Circle the number (1 is the lowest and 5 is the highest) you feel best describes your ability with each of the characteristics.

Honest	1	2	3	4	5
Vision-oriented	1	2	3	4	5
Inspirational	1	2	3	4	5
Competent	1	2	3	4	5
Communicate and listen well	1	2	3	4	5
Dependable (trustworthy)	1	2	3	4	5
Consistent	1	2	3	4	5
Self-confident	1	2	3	4	5
Fair-minded	1	2	3	4	5
Open to the ideas of others	1	2	3	4	5
Motivating	1	2	3	4	5
Assertive (not aggressive)	1	2	3	4	5
Recognize the positive behaviors and accomplishments of others	1	2	3	4	5
Problem solver/decision maker	1	2	3	4	5
Goal-oriented	1	2	3	4	5
Change-oriented	1	2	3	4	5
Effectively manage time	1	2	3	4	5
People-oriented	1	2	3	4	5
Able to deal with many issues	1	2	3	4	5
Seek knowledge	1	2	3	4	5

Total for each vertical column __ __ __ __ __

Add all five totals for your final score _____

Scoring:

80-100   You are an excellent leader with well-developed leadership skills.

60-79   You are a developing leader. With continuing experience and practice, you can make it to the highest level.

40-59   You are a manager who has not yet reached your leadership potential.

Below 40   You are a learner who needs to select areas of improvement and focus on strengthening them.

Do you have the self-confidence to seek the feedback of others?

It is important for you to evaluate yourself using the Leadership Proficiency Profile on the previous page, but it's also important to know how others see you.

Photocopy the Leadership Proficiency Profile (another copy is printed on the next page). At the next team meeting, give each of your team members a copy, and ask them to anonymously rate you. Give team members time to complete the profile while you are out of the meeting room. Ask an independent, nonpartisan observer to facilitate the process. As team members finish, ask the facilitator to collect and score the profiles. Ask for a final average for each of the twenty items as well as a total average.

Leadership Proficiency Profile

Directions: Rate your team leader on a scale of 1 to 5 (1 is lowest, 5 is highest) regarding each of the following leadership characteristics.

Honest	1	2	3	4	5
Vision-oriented	1	2	3	4	5
Inspirational	1	2	3	4	5
Competent	1	2	3	4	5
Communicate and listen well	1	2	3	4	5
Dependable (trustworthy)	1	2	3	4	5
Consistent	1	2	3	4	5
Self-confident	1	2	3	4	5
Fair-minded	1	2	3	4	5
Open to the ideas of others	1	2	3	4	5
Motivating	1	2	3	4	5
Assertive (not aggressive)	1	2	3	4	5
Recognizes the positive behaviors and accomplishments of others	1	2	3	4	5
Problem solver/decision maker	1	2	3	4	5
Goal-oriented	1	2	3	4	5
Change-oriented	1	2	3	4	5
Effectively manage time	1	2	3	4	5
People-oriented	1	2	3	4	5
Able to deal with many issues	1	2	3	4	5
Seeks knowledge	1	2	3	4	5

Total for each vertical column   __ __ __ __ __

Add all five totals for your final score   _____

Coaching/Counseling to Convey Expectations and Achieve Results

Now that you have a handle on the role of a strong leader throughout each stage of a team's development, here is a concept to keep in mind at all times:

Team members will accomplish what they are expected to. If expectations are high, then results will likely be achieved. If expectations are low, then results won't likely be achieved.

The team leader has a tremendous impact on how team members feel about themselves and how they feel about their ability to achieve.

Back in the 1920s, on a cold January night, an executive of the New York Telephone Company, Birch Forager, came out of a theater. Dressed in a tuxedo, he descended into a manhole. Asked why he did this he replied, "I knew a couple of my cable splicers were working down there, so I just dropped in on 'em to have a little chat."

In time, Forager became known as the "man of ten thousand friends." He made a habit of showing he cared about the company's employees. It was his way of showing he considered their jobs important.

"Great minds have purposes; others have wishes."

—Washington Irving

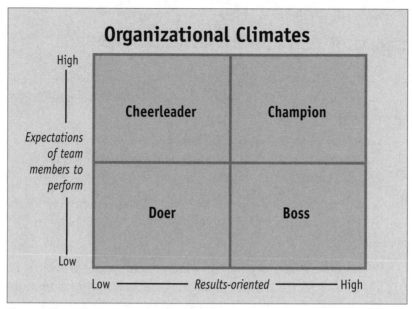

Fig. 12. *Team leader effectiveness grid.*

As the Team Leader Effectiveness Grid in figure 12 shows, there are four different "organizational climates" a team leader can create. The one to strive for is "Champion." Here is a summary of each climate:

1. The Doer (low expectations, low focus on results). In this type of climate, the team leader expresses low expectations of the team members. He or she delegates only menial or unimportant tasks rather than important ones that have greater rewards. Nor does the leader provide direction to set any goals. Results aren't valued. Maintaining the status quo is. The so-called leader becomes a "doer" rather than a coach and counselor. The team is left to fend for itself with little or no direction or feedback. They carry out the same old routine work with no attention to producing meaningful, quality results.

2. **The Boss** (high attention to results, low expectations of team members). The Boss is very results-oriented, but doesn't have high expectations of team members. He or she sets goals for the team, but without input and participation from members. This type of leader believes that team members must be told what to do and how. Further, this type of leader threatens team members who disagree with the goals and/or the methods for achieving them. Inherent in this leader's beliefs is that team members don't care or don't have the ability to define goals and carry out useful work. He or she believes that the team works only for extrinsic rewards, namely a paycheck, and doesn't care about intrinsic rewards such as recognition and belonging. Thus, the only feedback from the Boss is negative feedback when something goes wrong. If the team gets results, there is no feedback, just a paycheck.

3. **The Cheerleader** (high expectations, low focus on results). The team leader expresses high expectations of the team, but provides little or no direction. Many new team leaders can fall into this category because of their eagerness to please team members. They patronize and placate team members with trite phrases like "You can do it," "We're all in this together," and "We've got to pull together and work as a team." But these statements are hollow because there's no attention to goals and results. No one is held accountable. Team members start thinking, "Pull together and do what?" For a while, the team might feel good, but eventually frustration sets in because the team lacks focus.

4. The Champion (high expectations, high attention to results). The team leader truly "champions" the efforts of others. True leadership is exemplified. Remember, leadership is "the ability to help your team define what is important to accomplish (goals and priorities); to get results through coaching, counseling, and resources; and to help team members grow in the process." The Doer, the Boss, and the Cheerleader tend to be self-centered, power-oriented, or overpowering. The "champion" is team-centered and empowering. Always strive to be a real champion who enables a team to achieve and who expects team members to make decisions, solve problems, and grow through the team-building process. Even when you're operating in the more autocratic "Telling" role of team leader during the early stage of your team's development, you can make your expectations high and clearly convey that you believe team members can meet them. As your team matures and your role as leader evolves into coach and then counselor, you can empower members more and more.

"There can be no economy where there is no efficiency."

—Benjamin Disraeli

The Empowerment Concept

The word *empowerment* has been used so often—and so loosely—in business that many managers don't stop to consider what it really means.

Consider the word *power*:

- Power is the ability to influence or affect change.
- Power is the ability of one person to influence another.
- Power is having the authority and responsibility to get things done.

Empowerment, then, is the sharing of power from one person to another. Empowerment is the granting of influence and authority to take responsibility, influence change, and get important things done.

Empowerment is the gradual release of control of one person over another.

The continuum in figure 13 shows the stages of team development. As a team matures, it should be granted more influence and authority, just as a supervisor grants more autonomy to a proven employee or a parent gives a child more privileges.

Defining	Planning	Follow through	Transformation
Being controlled			Self-control

Fig. 13. *Teams earn more control as they mature.*

The key is this: power should be granted over time. Consider what happens to people who have had little or no power and then have it suddenly dumped in their laps. Many times they overcompensate and overuse their power. In other instances, they run from it, afraid of exerting their authority and influence and afraid to make mistakes and take responsibility.

Here are some ways a team gains more control and power as it moves from the defining stage to the transformation stage.

Powerless ———— to ————▶ Powerful

• Boss is responsible	• Team is responsible
• Waits for orders	• Creates its own orders
• Little influence in problem solving and decision making	• Influence to make decisions and solve problems
• Reactive	• Proactive
• Places blame	• Solves problems
• Status quo	• Creative
• Unmotivated	• Motivated

"Rank does not confer privilege or give power. It imposes responsibility."

—Peter Drucker

Gradually Releasing Power as Trust Builds

As team members demonstrate their maturity and responsibility, they should be rewarded with greater trust. Figure 14 depicts the gradual release of power as trust builds.

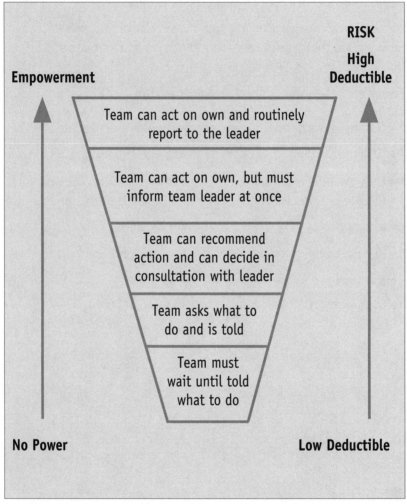

Fig. 14. *As trust among team members and the team leader builds, members are given more power, at greater risk to the leader.*

Dealing With Risk

Consider the analogy of purchasing an insurance policy. The lower the deductible the higher your cost, but your risk is lower in terms of potential loss.

The higher the deductible, the lower your cost is, but your risk goes up.

As a team leader, the more you share your power, the more you risk. You're betting your team can perform. You have a lower cost, in terms of the time you spend trying to maintain the team, since it manages itself.

The less you share power, the more control you have, so perceivably you risk less. Unfortunately, what you are likely to be insuring is mediocrity.

Risk and Its Relationship to Empowerment

People who are empowered must take responsibility for setting goals, solving problems, and making decisions. Of course, empowered people are responsible for the outcomes of their choices. All of this requires a willingness to take risks, and many people fear risk taking. Here are some basic guidelines for encouraging reasonable risk taking:

- **Set people up for success.** Help employees and team members get the resources they need to do their jobs. Train them. Communicate clearly with them.

- **Remove obstacles.** Don't create unnecessary rules and cumbersome reporting systems. If you do, team members will spend their time on bureaucratic matters rather than on getting results. They may also fabricate reports to protect themselves from risk.

- **Push them out of their comfort zone (gently).** People often want to play it safe. They can rationalize and find many reasons not to follow through. Usually they fear failure, which leads to the final point:

- **Coach people through mistakes; don't condemn them.** If people make mistakes, don't beat them up. Try to find out why they made the mistake and concentrate on fixing it. If people are blamed for their indiscretions, they learn not to make mistakes. In other words, they won't take risks. They'll play it safe and maintain the status quo.

Empowering a Continuous Improvement Team

Organizations often form continuous improvement teams, or project teams, to work on one particular task or to solve some specific problem. But just pushing the work downward does not necessarily ensure it will get accomplished. The team must understand what it is supposed to accomplish. Yet simply telling the team what to do likely won't get commitment. Team members must participate in goal setting, establishing standards, solving problems, and making decisions. In other words, a team must be empowered. The flowchart in figure 15 shows the empowerment process for an improvement or project team.

"Leadership is power, and how one perceives power is likely to influence how one behaves as a leader."

—Michael Maccoby, social psychologist

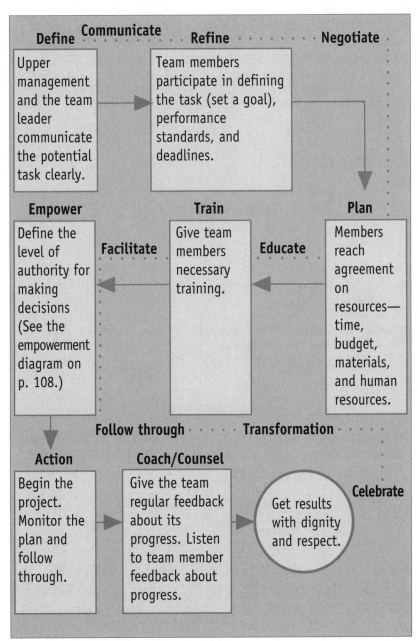

Fig. 15. *Team empowerment process.*

Real Power Is Win-Win

There are two ways to look at power. In the old style of management, power is a matter of *position*: I WIN, you LOSE.

The new style management focuses on personal power: I WIN, you WIN.

Positional Power

If you're a manager or team leader, *you have no power.* That's right. What you have is a *perception* of power. If you're called "manager" or "leader" or if you're listed above others on an organizational chart, it can be implied that you have more power than those below you on the chart. But just because you have more *perceived* power, will others automatically follow you? The answer is an emphatic *no.*

If positional power doesn't guarantee success in getting others to follow you, what does? *Character authority*, or personal power.

Personal Power

The most important traits of people with personal power are trust, honesty, an ability to inspire, openness, and a people-orientation. They are driven by values. People *choose* to follow leaders with personal power; they don't have to be forced to.

"If a man can accept a situation in a place of power with the thought that it's only temporary, he comes out all right. But when he thinks that he is the cause of the power, that can be his ruination."

—Harry S. Truman

A team leader with personal power shares power. He or she champions the efforts of others. In other words, the leader strives for *win-win* results. Team members and team leader alike benefit.

Team leaders who possess position power structure their authority around this theme: "My way, or the highway." Translated: "I win, you lose." If team members perceive that the team leader makes decisions and acts only for personal gain, then they aren't likely to truly follow that person. They will give the impression they are following, but really, they'll just do what they must do to keep their jobs and get a paycheck. They aren't working with commitment to the task or to the leader.

Team members who know they're working in a win-lose climate will sometimes sabotage the leader, the goals, and the tasks they're working on. This is referred to as the *social exchange theory*. It is essentially the same as the Golden Rule with a caveat added on.

> **Social Exchange Theory:** Do unto others as you would have them do unto to you, OR they will make it even in the end.

People want to be treated with respect, not manipulated, have power used over them, or have someone else achieve personal gain at their expense. Personal power (character authority) creates a win-win environment.

> *"There are but two powers in the world: the sword and the mind. In the long run, the sword is always beaten by the mind."*
> —Napoleon

What Motivates Team Leaders to Use Win-Lose

Test whether you have a tendency to use power over people instead of empowering people. Place an "X" on the continuum to indicate how strongly you tend to exhibit power-oriented (win-lose) behaviors.

1. Powerful people frequently act in strong and vigorous ways to display their power.

   Yes _____ No

2. Powerful people frequently think about ways to affect and change other peoples' behavior and feelings.

   Yes _____ No

3. Powerful people care considerably about their personal prestige, reputation, and position.

   Yes _____ No

4. Powerful people withhold information and knowledge from team members in order to use power over them.

   Yes _____ No

5. Powerful people take credit for team accomplishments rather than share credit and promote the accomplishments of team members.

   Yes _____ No

6. Power-hungry people silently compete against their teams and want others to fail.

Yes _____ No

7. Powerful people use position power as a threat to get others to perform.

Yes _____ No

8. Powerful people don't delegate important tasks to team members in favor of more ordinary tasks that are relatively unimportant and, therefore, less likely to be widely noticed by others in the organization.

Yes _____ No

9. Powerful people don't train team members and have a secret desire that they will make mistakes and fail.

Yes _____ No

"The measure of man is what he does with power."
—Pittacus

From Lethargy to Empowerment

Too often, so-called team leadership and empowerment has been a "pipe dream." There have been good intentions to empower team members, but under pressure, traditional management has stepped in and taken back control. In so doing, they limit problem solving, creativity, decision making, and the freedom of team members. The next several pages contain figures (see figs. 16-19) that illustrate four different levels of authority, from lethargy to empowerment, that can affect team performance.

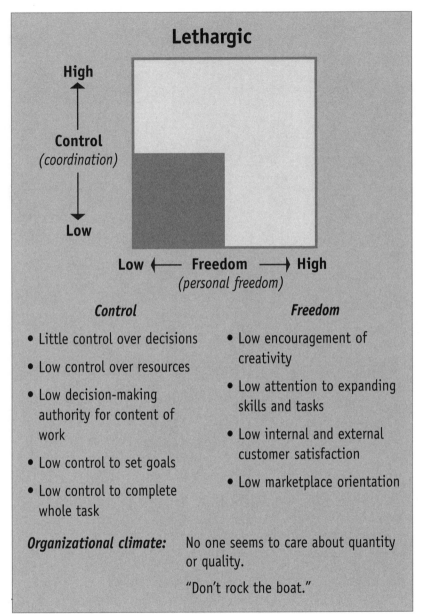

Lethargic

High ↑
Control
(coordination)
↓ **Low**

Low ←— **Freedom** —→ **High**
(personal freedom)

Control

- Little control over decisions
- Low control over resources
- Low decision-making authority for content of work
- Low control to set goals
- Low control to complete whole task

Freedom

- Low encouragement of creativity
- Low attention to expanding skills and tasks
- Low internal and external customer satisfaction
- Low marketplace orientation

Organizational climate: No one seems to care about quantity or quality.

"Don't rock the boat."

Fig. 16. *The Lethargic level is characterized by low team control and coordination and low personal freedom.*

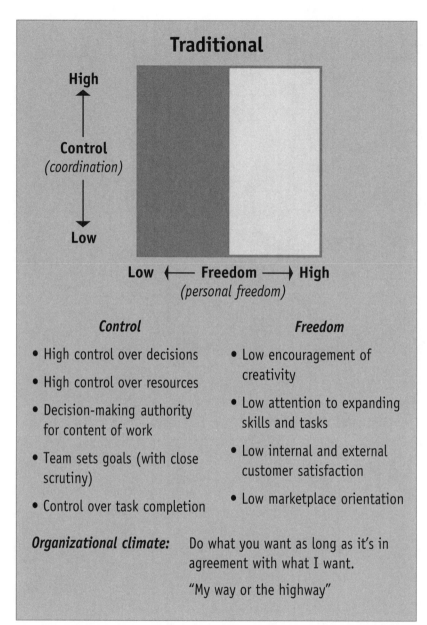

Fig. 17. *The Traditional level is characterized by high management control over the team and low personal freedom.*

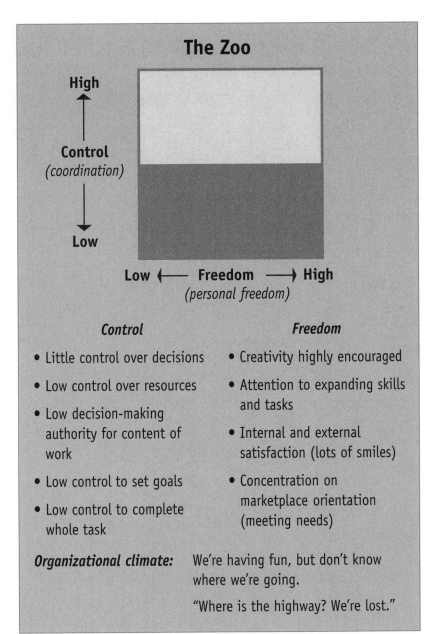

The Zoo

High

Control
(coordination)

Low

Low ←— Freedom —→ High
(personal freedom)

Control	*Freedom*
• Little control over decisions	• Creativity highly encouraged
• Low control over resources	• Attention to expanding skills and tasks
• Low decision-making authority for content of work	• Internal and external satisfaction (lots of smiles)
• Low control to set goals	• Concentration on marketplace orientation (meeting needs)
• Low control to complete whole task	

Organizational climate: We're having fun, but don't know where we're going.

"Where is the highway? We're lost."

Fig. 18. *The Zoo is characterized by low team control and coordination and high personal freedom.*

Empowered

The unshaded portion represents that there is always room for improvement. Thus, empowerment reflects a continuously improving climate.

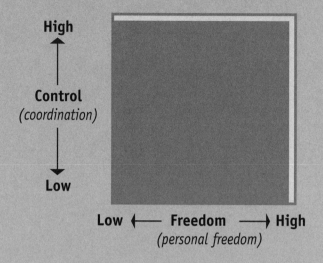

Control

- High control over decisions
- High control over resources
- Decision-making authority for content of work
- Team sets goals
- Control over task completion

Freedom

- Creativity highly encouraged
- Attention to expanding skills and tasks
- Internal and external satisfaction (lots of smiles)
- Marketplace orientation (meeting needs)

Organizational climate: We want you to have the control and freedom to be the best you can be.

"Be the best you can be."

Fig. 19. *The Empowered level is characterized by high team control and coordination and high personal freedom.*

How Much to Empower

Remember that empowerment is a process that occurs over a period of time. It is, to a great degree, based on the trust level and demonstration of success and results that occur because the leader and the team choose to work together. This chapter ends with an "Authority Progression Chart" that suggests which skills and tasks should gradually be shared with the team (see fig. 20).

You may or may not agree with the gradual release of all tasks listed on the progression chart. Pick and choose the tasks related to your team situation. Gradually empowering your team helps team members assume power and take responsibility. It is important for you, the team leader, to coach and counsel effectively through the process.

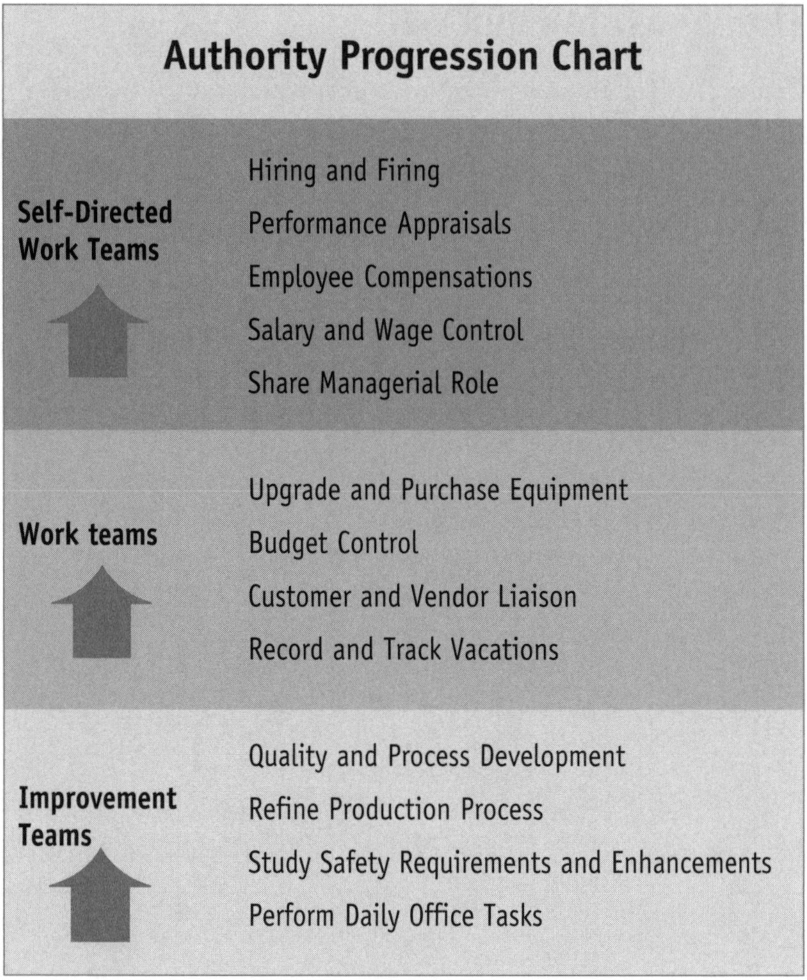

Authority Progression Chart

Self-Directed Work Teams

Hiring and Firing

Performance Appraisals

Employee Compensations

Salary and Wage Control

Share Managerial Role

Work teams

Upgrade and Purchase Equipment

Budget Control

Customer and Vendor Liaison

Record and Track Vacations

Improvement Teams

Quality and Process Development

Refine Production Process

Study Safety Requirements and Enhancements

Perform Daily Office Tasks

Fig. 20. *Tasks a team can gradually be given authority to perform as it matures.*

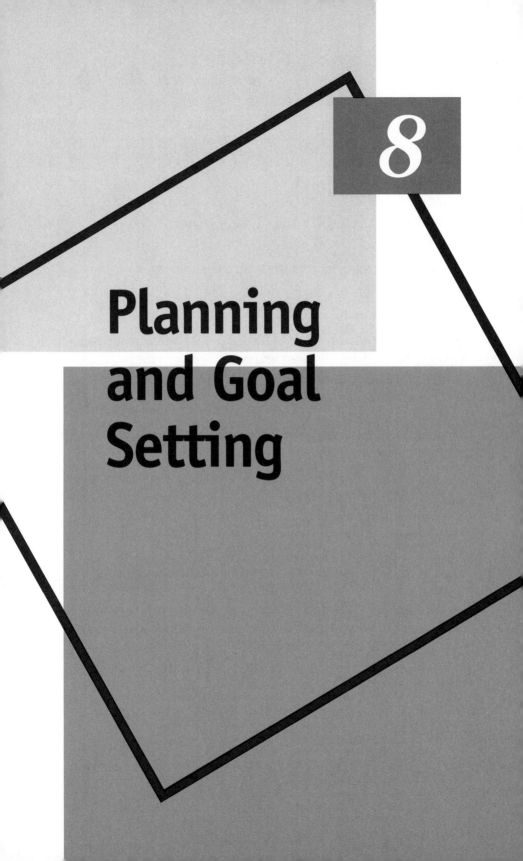

8

Planning
and Goal
Setting

> *"People who don't know what to do next almost always are those who don't have enough to do."*

—Dr. O.A. Battista

What Is Planning?

To understand team goal setting, it's important to know what planning is.

Planning is deciding in advance *what* to do, *how* to do it, by *whom* and *when.*

The key words in this definition are highlighted:

What (goal). One of the biggest mistakes new teams make is not defining their goals. And without goals, they don't know what they want to accomplish. The goal may not be communicated clearly or communicated at all. Or, each team member understands the goal differently. When this happens, there is heightened conflict and sometimes chaos. Having a clearly defined goal answers the question *what.*

Go slow to go fast. The development of goals and objectives and a plan to accomplish them should be a thought-provoking process that utilizes input from team members when possible. Each team member should leave a planning session with the questions what, how, whom, and when clearly answered. Such planning takes time. It can be a slow process. However, if done properly, planning can help the team avoid big problems later. Why? Because the team identifies, during the planning process, what it will be trying to accomplish and how it will be done. The team will start slowly, but will have the potential to go fast later because obstacles have been minimized during the planning process.

Some teams, unfortunately, *go fast to go slow*. That is, the team leader pushes the team to start doing something before members have defined what's important. The team may work on something unimportant that gets little, if any, results. The team dives into the work only to accomplish the wrong things.

Another scenario is that the team too loosely defines what it wants to accomplish, leaving too much open to interpretation. Or the team may define a goal, but neglect to devise a plan for accomplishing it, such as who is doing what by when. The team starts out fast only to be slowed down because the plan was not clear or perhaps not even developed. Always remember to *go slow to go fast*.

How (objectives). The how of planning is the "road map." If you're traveling by car from one city to another, you answer the question *what* by defining the city you're going to. But this doesn't tell you how to get there. For that you need a map showing the highways you must travel and what towns and cities you must go through. Objectives help you to know how you will accomplish your team goals. They become your road map. They define the step-by-step process to achievement. Team members are also more likely to willingly and enthusiastically accept the objectives if they participate in the planning process and have some say about what the objectives will be. In other words, they must help to develop the road map.

Who (team members). During the planning process, team members must commit to the plan by agreeing to work toward accomplishing the goal. Work assignments can be volunteered for or the team leader can delegate them.

When (deadlines). A goal and a plan (objectives) without a deadline is like getting on an airplane and having the pilot say, "Our destination is New York City, but I don't know when we'll arrive—maybe tonight, but then again, it could be tomorrow morning." Accomplishing a goal requires a commitment. Without deadlines, chaos reigns. Costs for human resources escalate because you don't know how long you need them, and team members don't know when their objectives are to be accomplished in relation to each other.

The Goal Setting/Planning Process

The goal setting and planning process necessary for effective team achievement and success can be effectively summed up with the DIAMOND acronym. (See fig. 21.)

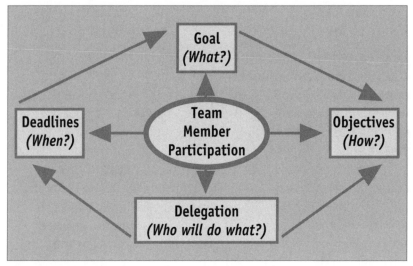

Fig. 21. *A goal is a "diamond in the rough."*

(Note: Compare this model to the Team Empowerment Process in fig. 15 to see the parallels.)

Here, using the acronym DIAMOND, are the key components of effective goal setting and planning.

Deadlines — They define time commitments.

Inclusion — Commitment comes from participation and ownership. Encourage team members to help define their own plan to achieve a goal.

Action-oriented — Once a goal and a plan are established, you must take action to implement them. These actions sometimes involve risk taking. However, good planning minimizes risk.

Measurable — Goals need to be measurable so the team can be held accountable. If you don't have quantifiable goals, you can't determine whether you're achieving anything.

Objectives — Remember that objectives are your road map. Step by step, they define what you will do to achieve your goal. You must decide with your team who will accomplish which objectives.

Negotiated — Give the team the opportunity to share in the decisions about what to do, how to do it, by when, and by whom. Team members must have the opportunity to negotiate for resources.

Delegated — Real delegation not only involves giving people responsibility to get results, but also the authority to make decisions and solve problems. Real delegation is empowerment.

Planning for Results!

There are three kinds of planning that teams get involved in:

1. **Reactive planning.** Actually, *reactive planning* is a contradiction in terms. It's listed here as a type of planning because sometimes teams develop a pattern of reacting to "the crisis of the day." Under the guise of planning, everyone on the team is called together. But rather than really planning, the team leader or someone with even more authority barks out orders, usually before anyone has bothered to get the facts regarding the crisis or emergency. When this happens frequently to teams, members become frustrated. They're always chasing the next crisis. Their motivation goes down and their stress level goes up because the priorities change everyday and they have no opportunity to provide input or to do real planning.

2. **Preactive planning.** This is the concept of planning the future based on the past. For instance, a team working on a project similar to one they've encountered in the past will base the plan for the new project on the former project. This type of planning is sometimes called *order of magnitude*. If the team starts a new project perceived to be twice as large as a past project of a similar nature, the team may just double the budget and performance standards or increase the magnitude.

   Preactive planning is better than no planning, but basing the future on the past can be dangerous. It assumes that past methods were accurate, efficient, and effective. Past experience can certainly be valuable, but only as an experiential factor in building a plan for the future.

3. Interactive planning. Interactive planning involves building the future the way *you* want it to be. It is also referred to as *idealized redesign*; that is, a team, in defining a goal and plan, should idealize about the outcome it wants. Team members can actively develop practical objectives to accomplish the goal. They may eventually have to change the idealized goal statement somewhat to make it achievable, but this is okay as long as it's done in the planning phase and not in the implementation phase.

Another way to look at interactive planning is to consider the concept of "zero-based plan building." The parallel to this is "zero-based budgeting," which means building a budget from scratch, based on what you really need, not based on what you spent in the past.

Zero-based plan building is developing a goal and a plan based on what your team really needs and wants to accomplish, rather than setting a goal based on what the organization has always done. Teams can get into the bad habit of setting the same goals year after year simply by changing a few numbers. Interactive planning calls for team members to set a goal that is fresh and then to figure out how to achieve it.

"At age 8, I set a goal to own my own restaurant. I figured if I owned it, I'd never be hungry, and I went hungry a lot. When I was 13, I got a job as a counterman. I was working fifty hours a week, working my way up. When I was 37, I finally opened my own restaurant—Wendy's. I didn't set out to have thousands of franchises. My goal was to make one restaurant work at a time. Goal setting made my life."

—Dave Thomas, founder of Wendy's restaurant chain

The Difference Between Goals and Objectives

As a business concept, goal setting has been around for a long time. It was particularly touted as a sound business practice in the 1960s and 1970s under the label of management by objectives (MBO). Perhaps the term should have been "management by goals and objectives" or MBGO.

As mentioned previously, there is a distinct difference between goals and objectives. Goals answer the question *what*. They determine your destination. Objectives answer the question *how*. They are the road map that tells you how to reach your destination.

Often the terms are used interchangeably, which can confuse team members. Obviously, teams should choose their destination and then use strategic planning to develop a road map.

You can use the word "goals" itself to remind you of the five criteria essential for effectively setting goals:

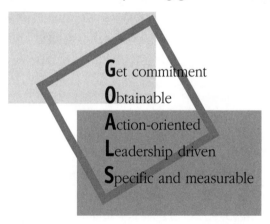

Get commitment

Obtainable

Action-oriented

Leadership driven

Specific and measurable

"Yard by yard, life is hard. Inch by inch, life is a cinch."

—Old proverb

What Keeps Teams From Setting Goals?

Although goal setting and planning are always important to project success, many teams fail to set goals. There are a variety of reasons for this, ranging from lack of training to fear of risk and failure. Here are ten of the most common obstacles to goal setting:

1. **Lack of management direction.** Sometimes, managers either don't want to take the time to guide the team or aren't sure what they think the team needs to accomplish. Remember that goals should be guided by customer feedback as much as possible. Managers can give their teams better direction if they stay close to their customers and elicit their feedback.

2. **Lack of training.** Team members sometimes just don't understand the goal-setting process and the purpose of strategic planning. And, unfortunately, they may never get the training they need to get started and then sustain the process.

3. **Fear of risk and failure.** The team may avoid setting goals because in the past when mistakes were made, employees were blamed, reprimanded, and punished instead of being coached. As a result, team members now find excuses not to set goals for fear the same thing will happen again.

4. **Fear of success.** Yes, it sounds strange, but some teams actually fear success because when they're successful, they get more work dumped on them. To be delegated work that is meaningful can be gratifying, but to be "dumped on" is not.

> *"One of the best ways of avoiding necessary and even urgent tasks is to seem to be busily employed on things that are already done."*
>
> —John Kenneth Galbraith

5. Goal setting makes people accountable. Some people don't want to be held accountable for their actions or for getting results and will go out of their way to avoid being "pinned down" to specific goals. Working on routine activities that may not be quantifiable or deadline-driven makes it harder for these people to be held accountable.

6. Goals force responsibility. Some people just don't want to take responsibility, preferring instead to let the team leader do so.

7. Impatience. This is a common problem. The team leader and members don't spend the time up front to set goals and plan because the process can be tedious. In their eagerness to plunge into the project, they neglect the most important step of all. The problem, of course, is that such teams may not achieve much because they really haven't defined what they want to do. Or they may work on the wrong things. The team becomes crisis-driven rather than goal-driven.

8. No established priorities. Team members can feel overwhelmed when there is too much to do but nothing is prioritized. Without clearly prioritized tasks and activities, team members may just "dive in" and start working, but without a clear sense of what needs to be done first to accomplish the overall goal. The situation is exacerbated when there is a lack of clear deadlines. Without deadlines, it is hard to prioritize.

9. Conflict. Team members may disagree about what to do, how to do it, and when to accomplish it. If there is too much disagreement and dissension, team members will likely either avoid dealing with the conflict or compete against each other.

10. Differing values about goal setting. Some people are very goal focused. Others concentrate more on building relationships. Some team members or the team leader may be more focused on the overall team climate. It may be that goal setting just isn't valued if too many people on the team would rather focus on other things. The exercise that follows will help you and your team members determine to what degree you value goals, individuals (relationships), and the team climate.

How Goal-Focused Is Your Team?

The following instrument will help you determine whether you and your team tend to be more goal-focused, relationship-oriented, or climate-centered. Obviously, all three areas are important, but different people value some areas more than others. First, complete the instrument yourself, then photocopy it to administer to your team.

Instructions

This is not a test with any right or wrong answers. It is a questionnaire you can use to describe team leader and team member values about goals, relationships, and organizational climate.

You will be given a brief statement of a situation and three possible attitudes you might have or actions you might take. Please rank order these attitudes or actions in terms of *how likely* you would be to take them, with a rating of "3" being the attitude or action you would *most likely take* and a rating of "1" being the attitude or action you would *least likely take*.

For each question, then, you should have three answers:

3 = The attitude or action you would *most likely* take

2 = The *next most likely* attitude or action

1 = The attitude or action you would *least likely take*

A. During a staff meeting, it is important for the leader to:

Keep focused on the task and goals at hand. (1) _____

Focus on team members' feelings and help them express their emotional reaction to the issue. (2) _____

Focus on the differing positions people on the team have and how the team members interact. (3) _____

B. A primary objective of a manager is:

Maintaining an organizational climate in which learning and accomplishment can take place. (4) _____

The efficient operation of the team. (5) _____

To help team members find themselves and be more aware of who they are. (6) _____

C. When strong disagreement occurs between you and a staff member, as the person in authority (and striving to achieve a certain goal), you:

Listen to the person and try to uncover where he or she might have misunderstood the goal-related activity. (7) _____

Try to get other team members to express their views as a way of involving them in the issue. (8) _____

Support the person for raising the question or disagreement. (9) _____

D. In evaluating team member performance, a team leader should:

Involve the team (i.e., department) both in setting goals and criteria for evaluation and in evaluating one another's performance. (10) _____

Try to objectively assess each team member's accomplishments and effectiveness. (11) _____

Allow team members to determine goals and criteria for evaluation. (12) _____

E. When two team members get into an argument, it is best to:

Help them deal with their feelings as a means of resolving the argument. (13) _____

Encourage other members to respond to the argument and try to help resolve it. (14) _____

Allow some time for expression by both sides, but keep in mind the overall goals and objectives and the task at hand. (15) _____

F. The best way to motivate team members who aren't performing up to their ability is to:

Point out to them the importance of the job to be done and their role in it. (16) _____

Try to get to know them better so you can understand why they aren't realizing their potential. (17) _____

Show them how their lack of motivation is adversely affecting other people. (18) _____

G. The most important element in evaluating a team member's performance is:

The person's technical skills and ability.   (19) _____

How well the person gets along with peers,   (20) _____
helps others learn, and gets work done.

The person's success in meeting self-   (21) _____
established goals.

H. In dealing with minority group issues, the team leader should:

Deal with the issues directly because they   (22) _____
threaten to disturb the atmosphere of the
organization.

Be sure that all members of the organization   (23) _____
understand the history of racial and ethnic
minorities in this country and the community.

Help members achieve an understanding of   (24) _____
their own attitude toward people of other
races and cultures.

I. A team leader's priority should be:

To make sure that all team members   (25) _____
have a solid foundation of knowledge and
skills that will help them become effective,
productive people.

To help team members learn to work   (26) _____
effectively in groups, to use the resources
of the group, and to understand their
relationships with one another as people.

To help team members become responsible   (27) _____
for their own education and effectiveness and
take the first steps toward realizing their
potential as people.

J. Routine team leader responsibilities:

Make it very difficult to adequately cover all (28) _____ the material that needs to be covered.

Keep team leaders from getting to know their (29) _____ team members as individuals.

Make it hard for team leaders to keep in touch (30) _____ with the climate and pulse of the organization.

1. Transfer your answers from the questionnaire to the scoring columns, placing a 1, 2, or 3 beside each question number.

2. Add up your totals for each column. The three totals combined should equal 60.

Scoring Columns

(The number in parenthesis matches the question response numbers.)

Goals	Relationships	Climate
(1) _____	(2) _____	(3) _____
(5) _____	(6) _____	(4) _____
(7) _____	(9) _____	(8) _____
(11) _____	(12) _____	(10) _____
(15) _____	(13) _____	(14) _____
(16) _____	(17) _____	(18) _____
(19) _____	(21) _____	(20) _____
(23) _____	(24) _____	(22) _____
(25) _____	(27) _____	(26) _____
(28) _____	(29) _____	(30) _____
Total _____	Total _____	Total _____

Now, mark your scores on the bar graph and fill it in.

Goals

Relationships

Climate

10   15   20   25   30

1. Which of the three values did you rate the highest?

_____

2. Which of the three did your team collectively rate the highest?

_____

3. What, if any, changes will you and your team make as a result of this analysis?

_____

Goal Priority and Planning Format

There are two primary considerations in establishing priorities:

1. Deadlines. Listing your goals and then writing in a deadline next to each one helps you determine which one is most *urgent.*

2. Potential payoff. Comparing the goals to each other in terms of perceived payoff will tell you which is most *important.*

One very important guideline to keep in mind is that once priorities are established, *they should not change* unless an emergency occurs. One of the most disconcerting and demotivating experiences for team members is to have a team leader or upper manager constantly change the priorities because of poor planning or politics.

The following is a template for prioritizing team goals. Use it to discuss your team's priorities over a given time, perhaps for the next six months to a year. Here's how to complete the template:

1. Working with your team, make a list of the team's top three to five priorities and list them in the first column.

2. Next, in column 2, rank each priority according to its importance, with 1 being most important and 5 least important.

3. In column 3, assign each priority a weighted value: 1=urgent, 2=less urgent, 3=not urgent.

4. Multiply column 2 by column 3—importance x urgency—to produce a raw score for each item.

"For everything you must have a plan."

—Napoleon

5. In the last column, place the priorities in rank order. The lowest score is your highest priority. The next lowest score is your next highest priority, and so on. If any of your raw scores tie, subjectively choose one over the other.

Priority	Importance	x	Urgency	=	Score	Ranking
1. ____	____	x	____	=	____	____
2. ____	____	x	____	=	____	____
3. ____	____	x	____	=	____	____
4. ____	____	x	____	=	____	____
5. ____	____	x	____	=	____	____

Once your team determines its priorities, you can rewrite them as goal statements that meet the DIAMOND criteria:

Deadlines

Inclusion (participation)

Action-oriented

Measurable

Objectives

Negotiated

Delegated

"There is no fate that plans men's lives. Whatever comes to us, good or bad, is usually the result of our own action or lack of action."

—Herbert N. Casson

Here's an example of a priority statement:

To reduce the number of accidents on our team

A priority statement doesn't meet the DIAMOND criteria. It's only a concept. It is, however, a start. To turn the priority into a goal, add a deadline and make it specific and measurable. The priority statement above can be rewritten as the following goal statement:

To reduce the number of accidents in our department from an average of four per month to zero by July 1.

Recall the definition of planning:

Planning is deciding in advance *what* to do, *how* to do it, by *whom* and *when.*

The chart on the next page incorporates the how, whom, and when into a strategic plan for the previous goal statement (what).

Objectives (How)	Deadlines (When)	Responsibility (Whom)	*Budget
1. Develop a safety training program, including video, workbook, and meeting dates	February 15	Dan McGuire	
2. Install nonskid ramps; hire outside company for installation	April 20	Gary Schirmer	
3. Upgrade lighting in total facility	April 20	Erin King	
4. Hire outside firm to clean floors and remove slippery substances	May 1	Tammy Schuman	
5. Develop a time/stress management training program to help employees stay more focused on their work	May 1	Dan McGuire	
6. Make safety shoes available at a discounted rate to all assembly line employees	May 10	Claude Burkhart	
7. Establish a safety award program for safety and accident improvement	May 15	Dana Embree	
*You may also want to add a column for budget.			

Figure 22 is a sample planning form that you may use as a model to assist your team in goal setting and strategic planning.

Strategic Planning Form

Goal (What): _____

_____

_____

Priority ranking _____

Objectives (How)	Deadlines (When)	Responsibility (Whom)	Budget
1.			
2.			
3.			
4.			
5.			
6.			
7.			
8.			
9.			
10.			

Fig. 22. *A sample strategic planning form.*

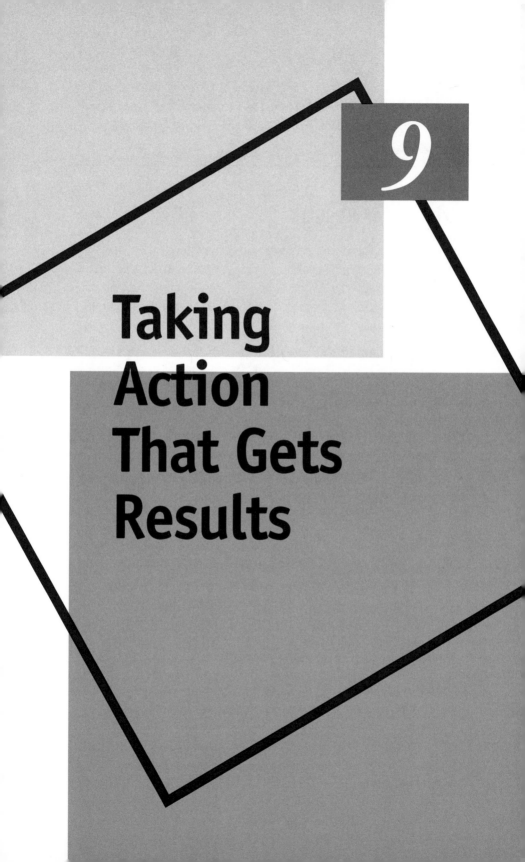

9

Taking Action That Gets Results

> *"Before you go to sleep, say to yourself, 'I haven't reached my goal yet, whatever it is, and I'm going to be uncomfortable and in a degree unhappy until I do.' When you do reach it, find another."*
>
> —Carl Sandburg

Striving for Results

There's a story about a cab driver and a minister who were waiting to get into heaven. The cab driver steps up to the Pearly Gates first. The Keeper of the Gate looks at his record down on Earth and says to the cab driver, "You may enter the Kingdom of Heaven and grab a silk robe and a gold staff."

The minister stepped up next. The Keeper of the Gate reviewed his record on Earth and proclaimed, "We'll let you in too, but you grab the cotton robe and the wooden staff."

The minister said: "I don't understand. I'm a man of the cloth. You let the cab driver in and gave him a *silk* robe and a *gold* staff. I don't understand.

The Keeper of the Gate looked the minister in the eye and said: "What we're interested in up here are results. When you preached, people went to sleep. When that cab driver drove, people prayed!"

The moral of the story? Take action and strive for results!

Have you ever been a member of a team that planned and planned and planned? Many times, teams get deluded into thinking they're achieving results just by planning. But planning is just a process of becoming. Results come from action. Meaningful action comes from a good plan.

In other words, planning is only a means to an end. The end is achieved when your team has accomplished the intended results.

Chapter 8 discussed ten common obstacles to goal setting. This same list also applies to implementing a plan, to actually taking action:

1. Lack of management direction
2. Lack of training
3. Fear of risk and failure
4. Fear of success
5. Goal setting makes people accountable
6. Goals force responsibility
7. Impatience
8. No established priorities
9. Conflict
10. Differing values about goal setting

Staying Action-Focused

If you're not moving forward, you're moving backwards. That's because your competitors *will* be moving forward, leaving you *behind*. Once you set goals and have a plan, *you must take action to get the desired results.*

The late Dr. W. Edwards Deming, who was instrumental in teaching the Japanese about Total Quality Management, used the PDCA method—Plan, Do, Check, Act—to define and explain planning and the need to be action and results-oriented.

"Find a direction and dedicate yourself to it, and remember that you can go as far as you want to go if you have a goal."

—Jim Marshall, former football player

Below is a modification of the PDCA process to help your team stay action-focused and goal-oriented.

Plan. As discussed in Chapter 8, define your goals clearly and develop a strategic plan for accomplishing them. A good plan always answers the questions what, how, who, and when. Whenever possible, the entire team or a representative of the team should be involved in the planning process.

Take action. Always set a "kickoff date" that marks when your team will begin processing the goal. Build this date into the plan. Be sure that team members clearly understand what they're trying to accomplish, have the needed resources, and have been trained to carry out their tasks and responsibilities.

Check performance. The team leader should monitor the achievement process. If problems arise or team members make mistakes, coach them through the mistakes rather than reprimand and punish. When team members perform well, it's important to immediately recognize their behavior. Doing so encourages more goal-focused, results-oriented achievement.

Act again. If mistakes are made, correct them. If problems develop, use the team to solve them. If decisions need to be made, make them. Keep the team action-oriented. It's easy to get bogged down in power struggles, unresolved conflicts, fear of failure, and politics. Don't let these obstacles keep you from moving forward.

If you don't find glaring problems and you're achieving success, start looking to the future. Consider the goals your team needs to set next as you strive for continuous improvement.

> *"Today, loving change, tumult, even chaos is a prerequisite for survival, let alone success.*
>
> —Tom Peters

Change: Don't Let It Immobilize Your Team

Quickly list three reasons why people won't accept change:

1. _____

2. _____

3. _____

Chances are, one of the reasons you listed was fear! Fear of change can keep teams from moving forward and taking action. Both team members and team leaders can conjure up all kinds of images about what could go wrong and the consequences of these mistakes. Maintaining the status quo is comfortable and safe. Unfortunately, staying put doesn't help you or your team to grow, nor is it likely to excite your customers very much. The next time you're inclined to freeze in your tracks because you fear change, consider this: Fear is just an acronym for *False Expectations Appearing Real.*

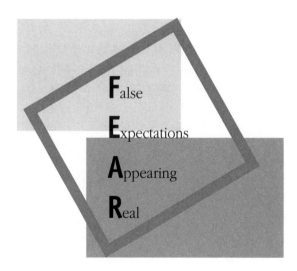

Beware of the boiled frog.

There's a concept called the Boiled Frog Syndrome. If a frog is put into a pot of boiling water, it will sense the heat immediately and jump out. If you put the frog into a pot of lukewarm water and turn the heat up gradually, the frog won't sense the change in the rising temperature until it's too late.

What's the point? The frog will be unaware of its environment heating up around it. It will be cooked before it knows it.

The analogy, of course, is that you may not be aware of the changes going on around you. If you and your company don't stay on top of those changes, then you too could, figuratively speaking, be boiled like the frog. Know when your environment is heating up, and be aware of what you need to change so that you and your team will continue to grow and prosper.

There are two critical factors in getting team members to accept changes:

1. **Whenever possible, involve the people who will be affected by the change.** The more team members understand an impending change, the more comfortable they'll be with it; therefore, they'll be more likely to embrace it. To thrust change on people without seeking their understanding and without giving them knowledge only asks for resistance. People resist what they don't know. In other words, fear of the unknown keeps people in their comfort zone.

Common Attitudes That Kill Progress

- "It won't work for our team."
- "We've tried that before."
- "It's too radical a change."
- "We don't have the time for it."
- "We're too small for it."
- "It doesn't fit our program."
- "We've never done it before."
- "You're two years ahead of your time."
- "Let's get back to reality."
- "That's not our problem."
- "Why change it? It's fine the way it is."
- "We're not ready for that."
- "Can't teach an old dog new tricks."
- "The Board would never go for it."
- "We've done okay without it."
- "Let's shelve it for the time being."
- "Let's form a committee."
- "Has anyone else tried it?"
- "It's against our policy."

2. **Always explain why change is necessary.** People need good reason to change. Change must make sense. The intended outcome must be better than what the team is presently doing. If team members are told to make a change just because the "boss" says so, they will subtly reject or sabotage the change.

To demonstrate, think back to when you were a child, maybe about eleven years old. On a Friday night, perhaps you went to your mother and asked, "Mom, could I go to the movies tonight?"

Her response? "No."

"But, Mom, why not?"

What was the answer you likely heard?

"Because I said so."

You were a child being treated like one. You didn't like it then, but you accepted it.

Now, what if you go to work tomorrow and find a memo on your desk that says: "Effective today we are changing our inventory procedures. See the instructions below and begin using the new forms attached to this memo."

This is a surprise to you. You were never informed of this change, nor was it ever discussed. So you go to your boss and ask, "Boss, why are we changing our inventory procedures?" What answer might you hear? "Because I said so!"

Now you're an adult being treated like a child. How do you accept this change? Probably not very well. You aren't given any reason for the change. More than likely your boss is using his or her power over you (do what I say) rather than empowering you (explaining the change and asking for your cooperation).

"On the plains of Hesitation bleach the bones of countless millions who, at the Dawn of Victory, sat down to wait, and waiting—died!
—George W. Cecil

As a team leader, remember this: If you don't involve team members in a change, you'll set yourself up for failure. Team members will prove the change should never have occurred in the first place.

Here are some additional strategies for introducing change to team members:

1. **Choose the right targets for change.** Help your team define what is most important to change. One mistake team leaders sometimes make is to try to change too many things at once. Remember, your strategy should revolve around continuous improvement, ultimately to meet your customers' needs. So, find out what your customers want you to change and focus on those key considerations.

2. **Make sure the timing is right.** Implement change when human resources and other resources are available. Set yourself up for success, not failure. Also consider what other goals and priorities your team is working on. Will team members have the time to devote to a new project or activity.

3. **Stay the course.** Once you set your priorities for change, see them through. (Recall the discussion on setting priorities in Chapter 8.) People won't take change seriously if they're always being told to make changes and then being told to disregard the new tasks or activities in favor of something else.

4. **Get input from the team.** Commitment comes from involvement. Involvement, of course, comes from participation. Discussing an impending change will help team

"Change is the only thing that offers new opportunity."
—Ross Shafer

members become more comfortable with the change and how it will affect them. People must see that the change makes sense.

5. **Choose the right people.** Sell proposed changes to the team members who are most open-minded and who have the greatest influence on other team members. If these people are willing to accept change, others are more likely to follow their lead.

6. **Facilitate each step.** Don't just drop change on people. Let your team know by your presence and participation that you are committed to whatever needs to change. Coach and counsel people through the change process. Recognize them for implementing changes, and coach them through mistakes.

7. **Circumvent the grapevine.** As discussed, fear of the unknown accompanies any change. People can conjure up all kinds of images of what can go wrong. When they talk to each other, they may exaggerate the negative scenarios. This fear and negativity can spread like wildfire through the team if left unchecked. Observe team members who are asked to make changes, be available to answer their questions, and allow them their fears—but keep them focused on the positive.

Famous Nay-Sayers

"Everything that can be invented, has been invented."
>—Charles Duell, Director of U.S. Patent Office, 1899

"Who the hell wants to hear actors talk?"
>—Harry M. Warner, Warner Brothers Pictures, 1927

"Sensible and responsible women do not want to vote."
>—Grover Cleveland, 1905

"There is no likelihood man can ever tap the power of the atom."
>—Robert Millikan in 1903, 1923 Nobel Prize winner in Physics

"Heavier than air flying machines are impossible."
>—Lord Kelvin, President, Royal Society, 1895

"Ruth made a big mistake when he gave up pitching."
>—Tris Speaker, baseball player, 1921

Delegating Team Members to Action

If you want your team to take action and get results, you must learn how to effectively delegate.

As discussed in Chapter 1, team members should be given a level of authority based on how well the team has taken responsibility and how well the team has earned the team leader's trust. (See fig. 23.)

Here are some key points to keep in mind as you delegate to team members:

1. **Always have a clear idea of what you want as an end result of the delegation.** One huge problem for teams is that they sometimes don't understand why they exist or what they should be working on. Communication from upper management and/or the team leader is vague. The overall goal and individual tasks need to be clear and specific. The scope of the work—as well as deadlines and responsibilities—need to be defined.

2. **When possible, decide together.** People are more likely to be committed to achievement if they are involved in defining the work.

3. **Authority must accompany responsibility.** Team members need to have the power to make decisions and solve problems. Remember, power is the ability to influence outcomes. Team members must know what level of authority they can assume. The accompanying chart suggests the level of authority a team leader may give a team or certain team members when delegating responsibilities.

Level of Authority	Trust	Empowerment
	Low	Low
• Team must wait to take action until told what to do		
• Team may make suggestions but team leader makes final decision		
• Team may make recommendations and then take action		
• Team may feel free to act independently but must keep team leader informed		
• Team may act on own, with periodic reports to team leader		
	High	High

Fig. 23. *Level of authority teams have when delegated assignments correspond to level of trust established.*

"You do not get paid for coming to work. You get paid for making things better."

—Tom Peters

4. Resources must accompany goals and tasks. Team members must have enough time, people, budget, and materials to do the job. If they don't, you set them up for failure right from the start. When you delegate a task, discuss the resources needed right at that time. Create a verbal, if not written, contract that outlines what the team member(s) will agree to do or accomplish, as well as the resources that will be provided.

Remember, the only way to get results is to take action. Helping team members overcome fear of change and delegating effectively are two ways to spur activity. One obstacle that can keep a team from moving forward is performance problems. The next chapter discusses ways an effective team leader can coach and counsel members through rough spots in performance and keep the entire team moving forward.

"We are not capable of everything."

—Virgil

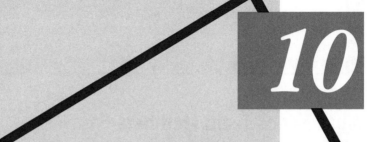

10

Dealing With Performance Problems

> *"All problems become smaller if, instead of indulging them, you confront them. Touch a thistle timidly and it pricks you; grasp it boldly, and its spine crumbles."*
>
> —William S. Halsey

What Keeps Team Members From Accomplishing?

Sometimes, on the way to getting results, performance problems arise that can frustrate both team leaders and team members. If you don't deal with these problems directly, finger pointing may start, rumors may circulate, and bad habits may become the norm.

Figure 24 suggests that team member performance problems fall into three general categories:

1. Environment problems (usually lack of resources)

2. Skill/knowledge problems

3. Motivational problems

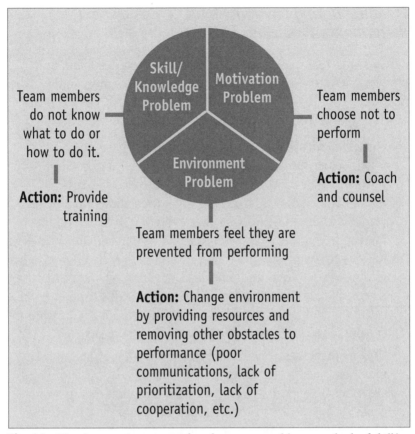

Fig. 24. *The three main causes of performance problems are lack of skill/knowledge, environment, and lack of motivation.*

Too often when things go wrong, people are blamed and, sometimes, made to feel stupid. However, there's usually an underlying cause that *can* be dealt with or corrected, if you give it the attention it needs in time.

"A teacher can only lead you to the threshold of your own mind."
—Kahlil Gibran

Troubleshooting Environmental Causes of Performance Problems

Rarely is the real reason for a team performance problem an unwillingness to do the job. Usually the cause is more subtle. The next time your team experiences performance problems, consider whether one of the following could be the cause:

- **Miscommunication and unclear direction.** These are listed together because they're interrelated. Many performance problems boil down to faulty communications. Team members sometimes have different expectations than team leaders. You can make sure that everyone's expectations are in sync if you follow through on one of the primary themes of this book: Teams are likely to perform well if they know what to do, how to do it, and who is to do what by when. In other words, clearly communicate these expectations to your team members and make sure they understand them if you want to cut down on performance problems and mistakes.

- **Lack of resources.** The four important resources team members need to do a quality job that meets customer needs are time, budget, materials, and people. Team members can easily be blamed for problems that are beyond their control when they don't have the resources they need.

- **Too much to do.** When team members have too much to do, they rush. They try to do more in less time. As a result, mistakes increase and eventually there are widespread performance problems because people start to burn out. Help team members by defining and then not changing priorities. Stay aware of the team's workload.

- **Lack of cooperation from others.** Team members may consciously or subconsciously compete with each other. They may withhold information, deliberately set traps for others, or provide misleading information. Team leaders need to set the tone for cooperation by creating a helping climate—one in which team members share information, are open to suggestions, and help each other achieve the mutually agreed upon goals. If you demonstrate these attitudes yourself, team members are likely to follow your example.

Troubleshooting the Skills/Knowledge Causes of Performance Problems

Too often when a job needs to be done, team leaders use "the first warm body through the door" method of selection. Team leaders who use this method create more problems than there were when the job was unfilled. In the quest to hurry up and get the job done, selecting the right people for the job can be overlooked. The people selected may be skilled, knowledgeable, and educated, but not necessarily in the right areas. Pay close attention to your skill needs when interviewing and selecting team members.

If team members are delegated goals and tasks without adequate training, mistakes are likely to increase. As mistakes increase, team members get frustrated and start hiding their mistakes to keep from exposing their "inadequacies." Some people struggle on, hoping they'll eventually be able to overcome their deficiencies. Some do, but many don't. Team leaders can minimize the problem by adequately training and developing team members for their jobs.

Particularly problematic are situations in which teams are formed, but little or no training is provided about the team process itself. In these cases, team members may not only lack technical skills training but human relations training as well. As a result, mistakes rise, and conflict and competition among team members increases.

When people haven't worked together before on teams, they may have difficulty understanding team building, dealing with conflicts, the dynamics of problem solving and decision making, dealing with change, and other issues. Asking people to work on teams often means asking them to work differently than they have before. Without training, it can be difficult for them to bond and accomplish goals.

Some of the key reasons to train teams, then, are these:

- To improve skills
- To increase productivity
- To increase effectiveness
- To improve efficiency and reduce cost
- To reduce stress by minimizing mistakes
- To promote team harmony
- To eliminate the "we've always done it this way" mentality and encourage receptivity to change

Let's make one thing very clear: It's never too late to assess your team's training needs. The best way to determine the training your team needs is to ask team members themselves. The team Training Needs Assessment in figure 25 will help you identify legitimate training needs. Make copies of the instrument and ask team members to complete it.

One of the most important aspects of using a training needs assessment is how to follow up on the information you obtain. Too frequently companies conduct needs assessments and then do nothing with the data. The results? Employees don't take management seriously and become frustrated.

Team leaders need not only to express to the team that the information will be used but also to provide a training plan so that team members can receive continuous training.

SAMPLE
Training Needs Assessment

The following interpersonal relations and technical skills training topics would be of assistance to our team. Please indicate your top three choices with a check mark:

- ☐ Team building
- ☐ Goal setting
- ☐ Strategic planning
- ☐ Conflict management
- ☐ Problem solving
- ☐ Creative thinking
- ☐ Supervisory skills
- ☐ Conducting performance reviews

- ☐ Project management
- ☐ Customer service
- ☐ Total Quality Management
- ☐ Time management
- ☐ Meeting management
- ☐ Stress management
- ☐ Dealing with change
- ☐ Communication skills

Please indicate any other training areas you think should be addressed:

_____

_____

_____

What specific skills training would help you and your team members do your jobs more effectively?

_____

_____

Name (optional) _____

Department _____

Fig. 25. *Sample Training Needs Assessment.*

Here are some key points to consider as you use a training needs assessment to develop a training program:

- **Training does not come free.** Management must make a financial commitment to training.

- **Look for trends.** Review data from your training needs assessment to determine what kind of human relations and technical skills training is needed most. Quite simply, tally how often each topic is check marked to help you rank order the training needs of your team.

- **Follow up with personal interviews.** After determining which training topics are most important for your team, meet with informal team leaders, those who are respected by the team, to elaborate on the needs assessment results. Gain their perspective about the results and what specific content areas training needs to address. The team members usually have a pulse on what's happening with the team and what they really need to do their jobs effectively.

- **Define specifically what training courses you will be able to deliver and when they can be delivered.** Set up a training schedule. Determine dates for training seminars. Some may need to be recurring since not all team members may be able to attend at the same time. If possible, make attendance voluntary. When training is forced, team members can be resentful. Market the training courses in such a way that employees want to attend.

- **Select trainers who can deliver quality programs.** One of the biggest mistakes companies and organizations make is to try to deliver training as cheaply as possible. They hold "train the trainers" sessions for staff who don't have platform skills. Although these so-called trainers may have a thorough knowledge of the subject, they may not be able to deliver it with interest, excitement, and enthusiasm. Select trainers wisely. If no one on your organization's staff can deliver the training, consider using outside agencies, independent speakers, and seminar companies.

Weighing the Cost of a Poor Trainer

To save money, a company will sometimes use an internal "trainer." Often, these trainers have no speaking skills, however, and training participants leave the training session feeling as if they've learned nothing. Often, then, companies end up spending more money on these types of training sessions than they would have if they'd hired a professional to begin with. Just consider this example: A company puts twenty-five team members in a room with an average hourly salary of $20 an hour for six hours. That expenditure equates to $4,500 per day ($20 an hour x 6 hours=$180 x 25 team members=$4,500). If the audience is bored to tears, the company has wasted its money. Hire qualified professionals to provide training.

- **Assess the value of the training.** Be sure to provide an evaluation form for each team member to fill out for each training session. These evaluations give team members an opportunity to indicate what they thought was meaningful about the training and what should be changed or deleted. Be sure to act on this feedback.

"Learning is the new form of labor. It's no longer a separate activity that occurs either before one enters the workplace or in remote classroom settings ... Learning is the heart of productive activity."

—Shoshana Zuboff

Dr. Malcolm Knowles is one of the key authorities on the subject of adult training. You may want to consider some of his key points as you develop and present training programs:

- **Adults have past experience.** Don't be condescending. Unlike children, adults aren't always bright-eyed and intent on soaking up knowledge. Fortunately, some are. Whether or not they are interested in the training, always strive to make the training interesting. *Involve* participants. Tap into their knowledge. Give them an opportunity to share with other team members and to learn from them.

- **Adults learn what they perceive they need to know.** In other words, they'll tune in if the training makes sense to them. They may tune it out if it doesn't. That's one reason it's so important to have qualified trainers. They can present information in a way that makes sense and is practical to the participants. As you plan training sessions, pay close attention to the content. Make sure it's meaningful and useful to most team members.

- **Adults want information they can use now.** Don't overload training sessions with theory and philosophy. Participants want to be able to apply what they learn immediately. Challenge team members by asking them to identify what behaviors and practices they plan to change. Concentrate on practical application.

- **Adults have greater self-confidence than children.** Plan training programs that encourage attendees' active participation and involvement. But never force team members to participate. Some may be shy or feel ill at ease. The primary point is that adults with experience and self-confidence will want to participate, so give them the opportunity to express themselves.

Troubleshooting Motivational Causes of Performance Problems

Actually any of the environmental or training issues previously discussed in this chapter can contribute to a lack of worker motivation that results in performance problems. Addressing these issues as suggested will significantly improve morale and motivation. Still, there are a couple of other reasons to consider when lack of motivation is an issue:

- **Lack of commitment.** If people aren't committed to what they're doing, they will make more mistakes. Lack of commitment can stem from a number of possible causes, including boring work, no vested interest, no opportunity to participate in defining the work, repetitive tasks, burnout, and lack of direction. Probably the most important factor for gaining commitment from people is to involve them in defining the work. If they help decide what needs to be done, they'll feel an ownership of the task and have stronger interest in getting the job done right.

- **Lack of work ethic and motivation.** Some people just don't value work. These people work to earn a paycheck, but that's all. People who don't value work are less likely to concentrate on their jobs and are, therefore, more likely to make mistakes. It's important to hold such team members accountable and to coach them regularly.

"Money spent on the brain is never spent in vain."

—Joe Griffith

Effectively Coaching and Counseling Team Members With Performance Problems

As discussed in Chapter 6, a team leader must be an effective coach, counselor, and facilitator. Recall the difference between coaching and counseling/facilitating. Coaching implies more talking. Counseling/facilitating entails more listening. Review the coaching, counseling, and facilitating techniques discussed in Chapter 6 and then apply them to the following exercise.

"As I grow older, I pay less attention to what men say. I just watch what they do."

—Andrew Carnegie

Dealing With Team Members Who Choose Not to Perform

Read the following case study and then outline below what you would say to the employee. Keep in mind the need to have effective coaching and counseling skills.

Case Study: A member of your customer service team has shown resistance to learning the new computerized inventory system. Other members of the team are becoming resentful of picking up her workload in order to meet customer requests. The team member in question has been well trained. She's also been given the resources to do her job well, and has received feedback and recognition when she has performed admirably.

Unfortunately, her unwillingness to learn the new program has become a problem.

As the team leader/supervisor, you must confront her with the problem. How would you handle this situation?

_____

_____

_____

_____

_____

_____

_____

_____

The Behavior-Focus Approach

Here is a ten-step technique, called the "behavior-focus" approach, aimed at focusing on the problem, not the person. The emphasis is on helping team members to change, not on punishing them for mistakes. It's important to make team members accountable, but a good team leader has the skills to help people change and grow. As you read each step, you'll see how it can be applied to the case study in the exercise you just completed.

Step 1:   Confront assertively, not aggressively.

Step 2:   *Pinpoint* the problem as you see it.

Step 3:   State the consequences of the problem.

I've noticed a hesitancy on your part to learn our new computerized inventory system. I'm concerned because others are having to assume your workload, and I believe our quality of service to our customers is slipping.

Step 4:   Get the facts and/or perspective of the team member.

It would help me to know why you've resisted learning this new program.

Step 5:   Pause and listen.

Step 6:   Ask the team member for potential solutions to the problem.

How would you suggest increasing your knowledge of the program?

Step 7: Note the suggestions.

I understand that you will enroll in a software course and that you will spend time working with the software tutorial included with the program. Does that sound acceptable to you?

Step 8: Document the suggestions chosen for change.

Step 9: Follow up by observing whether behavior is changing.

If it is, provide recognition. If not, provide further coaching and counseling and continue to document lack of performance.

Step 10: Eventually, one of two things will happen: the person changes his or her behavior and the problem is solved, or the person chooses not to change.

If the team member changes, reinforce the new behavior. If not, you have no choice but to ask the person to leave. If you have followed the steps accurately, you will have documented the poor performance.

The Do's and Don'ts of Performance Feedback

Remember, when giving feedback to team members who are having performance problems, the focus should be on helping them overcome problems and mistakes. The chart on the next page distinguishes the positive approach from the negative one.

Positive	Negative
1. **Focus on problem:** "I see a concern that we need to deal with.	1. **Focus on person:** "How could you do something so stupid?"
2. **Specific and based on analysis and observation:** "I have noticed that your reports have been late for three of the last four weeks."	2. **Generalized and based on emotion:** "You're always late with your reports."
3. **Assertive:** "I need your help in solving this problem."	3. **Aggressive:** "You need to get your act together and get these reports in on time.
4. **Focused and helpful:** "I feel that if you can get the reports done on time it will help both of us analyze the data and be more responsive to our customers."	4. **Threatening and punishing:** "If you can't do your job effectively and get the reports in on time, I'll find someone who can."

The tone you set will get either cooperation or defensiveness. Help team members to grow and change by coaching and counseling them through their mistakes and performance problems.

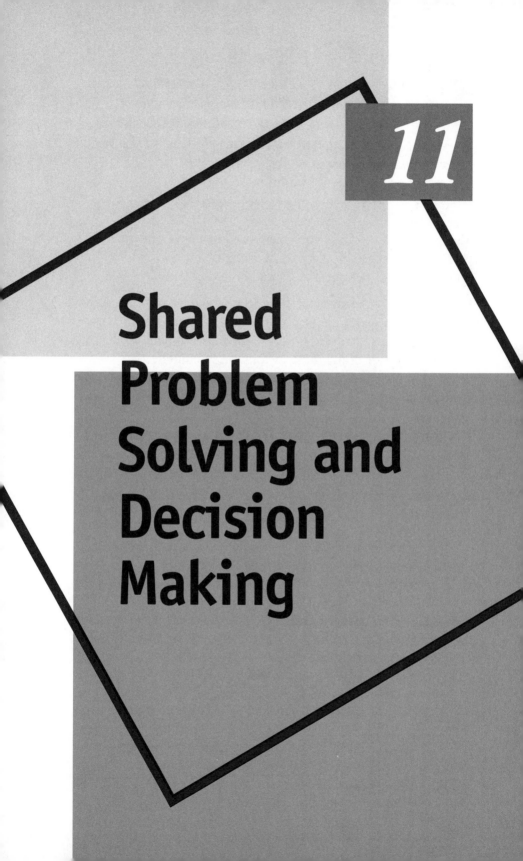

11

Shared Problem Solving and Decision Making

> *"The mere formulation of a problem is far more essential than its solution, which may be merely a matter of mathematical or experimental skills. To raise new questions, new possibilities, to regard old problems from a new angle requires creative imagination and marks real advances in science."*
>
> —Albert Einstein

All teams are or should be problem-solving teams. They play a vital role in the continuous improvement of goods, services, procedures, and people. Thus, they solve problems.

Problem solving is a dynamic process that involves people, facts, emotions, unknowns, conflict, distortions, competition for who has the best idea, analysis, observation, and communication. Yet the sheer number of the these factors can inhibit effective decision making and problem solving. Strong, effective leadership is essential. The team leader needs to set the tone.

Problem-Solving and Decision-Making Alternatives

There are essentially three ways teams can solve problems and make decisions:

1. Unilateral

2. Total team

3. Interface

Which method to use depends to a large extent on the team's maturity level, the type of decision to be made, and how quickly the decision must be made.

Unilateral

In unilateral decision making, the team leader decides without getting input from team members. This method is used when problems must be solved or decisions must be made very quickly. However, the team leader should always inform the team about the decision and why a particular alternative was selected to solve the problem.

Total Team

In total team decision making, the entire team is involved in the problem-solving process. This method works best when the team is no larger than about eleven people. If the team is much larger, there may be too many perspectives and opinions, which may lead to unnecessary conflict. Of course, the advantage to total team problem solving and decision making is that everyone gets to participate and contribute. The team is likely to arrive at better solutions because problems are scrutinized from several perspectives.

Interface

The interface method is essentially a democratic method. This method is suited for large teams where it would be unwieldy for every member to participate. Instead, selected members represent the entire team. These team members bring the ideas and suggestions of their constituents to the table. They also keep the team members they represent informed about decisions that are made and problems that are solved. All team members should eventually have the opportunity to be an interface representative.

"I do not believe in a fate that falls on men however they act; but I do believe in a fate that falls on them unless they act.

—G.K. Chesterton

What Keeps Teams From Solving Problems?

Sometimes, teams become immobilized and feel incapacitated to make decisions and solve problems. Here are some of the obstacles that prevent teams from solving problems:

Fear. As discussed in various chapters in this book, fear of failure and fear of the unknown can bring problem solving to a screeching halt. Team members need to be supported throughout the problem-solving process, rewarded for good decisions, and coached through decisions that aren't effective. That leads to the next point.

Lack of management support. If a team feels that management won't support its solutions to problems, members will do one of two things: put off making decisions and solving problems or make safe decisions.

Politics. Team members may feel that if they don't make the "right" decision politically, they won't be supported. Teams need to know they will be supported through unpopular decisions.

Competition. Team members may compete against each other for the best solution to a problem. This can become a very destructive process. If team members start taking sides, the team becomes polarized and compromise becomes next to impossible to achieve. Teams need to be encouraged to compete—on the outside, against their real competition—not internally.

Conflict. Conflict is related to competition. Competition can lead to conflict. It is the "my idea is better than your idea" mind-set. Team members must be encouraged to listen to and be open to the ideas of their teammates and to strive to get beyond their differences.

"If you do nothing, you're doing wrong."
—Lord Mountbatten

Too many alternatives. Some problems may have numerous solutions. When that happens, team members may become confused and unable to sort through the alternatives. If there is no systematic method in place to sort through the possibilities, the team may procrastinate. (The problem of too many alternatives is addressed in step 5 of the rational problem-solving process discussed later in this chapter.)

Lack of leadership. Without leadership, a team will likely have no focus. Team members do their own thing or nothing at all. An effective team leader keeps the team focused in spite of conflict, controversy, or too many alternatives.

Lack of facts. The team feels it can't make decisions or solve problems because it lacks facts. Sometimes this can be a convenient excuse to put off problem solving. Teams need to be proactive and seek out the facts. With facts, they can likely get to the root causes of a problem.

Impatience. In our fast-paced society, people often associate quicker with better. In fact, quick, fast, lightning-speed problem solving and decision making is often highly valued. But if decisions aren't thought through and substantiated with facts, team members may later have to "fix" their mistakes.

Lack of familiarity and trust. Team members may not know each other well enough or feel comfortable enough with each other to contribute to the problem-solving process, particularly if the team is in the forming (defining) or norming (planning) stage. The team leader needs to nurture team relationships. Teams solve problems more efficiently if they understand each other. However, in the extreme, this can lead to the next problem.

Too much familiarity. In this situation, team members know each other so well they take each other for granted. They may filter the messages of fellow team members, assuming they know what those members are saying. Or they may be too blunt in disagreeing with each other since they feel they know each other so well. In this case, the team leader needs to remind team members of the need to respect each other.

Lack of resources. Team members will become unmotivated quickly if they feel that no matter what decisions they make or solutions they come up with for problems, they won't have the resources necessary to implement and carry them out. The team leader needs to help team members weigh alternatives to determine whether resources are available to support their decisions.

Decision-Making and Problem-Solving Techniques

The Rational Problem-Solving Process

As noted at the start of the chapter, problem solving is a dynamic process, and the team leader plays a key role in setting the tone for that process. Here are the key steps:

1. **Identify the real problem.** The emphasis here is on the word *real*. Team members who get in a hurry and lose patience often identify symptoms rather than problems. And when they define symptoms, they often concentrate more on who created the problem rather than on what the problem is. If the emphasis is on who, the problem likely won't be solved. If you look deeper, you'll usually find that the directions were never clear, resources were inadequate, leadership was lacking, or some other problem was the culprit. Look for *real* problems. If, after analyzing the problem, you discover that the person is the problem, then coach and counsel as suggested in Chapter 10.

2. **Gather the real facts.** Don't jump to conclusions. Quick, emotional decision making that's not based on facts can be costly and can result in hurt feelings and poor relationships. When trying to solve problems, *ask more questions and do more listening.*

3. **Propose a solution.** Someone on the team must take a risk by being the first one to propose a solution. How others respond to that person and the proposed solution will likely determine the level of participation by others. If the first team member who speaks up is recognized positively for his or her idea—a simple "thanks for your idea" will do—then others will likely contribute their ideas.

   If others put down the first team member's suggestion with statements like, "That will never work here," "We've tried that before," "That'll never fly," or something similar, it will teach the person who spoke up to stop making suggestions. Likewise, others on the team will get the same message, and no one will be willing to risk offering possible solutions. In this scenario, team members learn it is safer to keep their mouths shut, speaking up only when they feel their suggestions aren't controversial. As a result, the best ideas may never see the light of day.

4. **Encourage alternative solutions.** As mentioned, the team leader must create a climate where all ideas are encouraged and listened to. The team leader sets the tone by recognizing and rewarding people for their ideas and potential solutions to problems.

5. **Select the best alternative.** How do team members know what the best alternative is? They don't! All the team can do is weigh the alternatives. With good coaching from the team leader, team members can select the best three or four alternatives. They can then look at potential outcomes for each alternative, and determine which solution is likely to produce the best results.

6. Take action! As discussed in Chapter 9, teams will often plan but never get around to taking action. The same thing can happen in the problem-solving process. Team members become concerned that their best alternative is not good enough. Or the team may suffer from "analysis paralysis." It is safe to analyze. The team can't make mistakes; however, it can't experience success either. The team leader must push the team out of its comfort zone and then coach, counsel, and support the team through its actions.

7. Evaluate the decision. As soon as the team takes action, the team leader and members should begin analyzing the alternative they chose. They need to know whether it's producing the anticipated outcome and results. If so, they can keep moving forward with that decision. If the alternative isn't yielding the intended results, the team needs to meet again to look at other alternatives. There's nothing wrong with admitting they made a wrong decision if they do it early enough to correct it. Further problems develop when the team won't admit mistakes or ignores problems.

The Group Dynamics of Brainstorming

As discussed in the seven-step rational problem-solving and decision-making model, the team leader sets the tone. The group dynamics are affected by the team leader's willingness to create an open climate in which ideas are encouraged. Brainstorming is an excellent tool for encouraging the free exchange of ideas and solutions. The team leader and members should keep the following brainstorming rules in mind:

1. Team members should suggest every idea they can think of, no matter how unpractical it may seem.

2. No suggestion should be discussed or criticized until all ideas are out on the table.

3. Everyone on the team must be given an opportunity to suggest ideas, although no one should be forced to participate.

4. Appoint someone to write all ideas on a flip chart, as they are suggested.

5. Group any suggestions that are the same.

6. Discuss and evaluate.

7. Make a choice.

Nominal Group Technique: Another Problem-Solving Alternative

Nominal Group technique is a way to solve problems and make decisions without getting immersed in controversy and conflict. It can help a team to make a choice when there are several meaningful alternatives.

For example, if a quality improvement team is trying to minimize and prevent accidents within the facility, they may first brainstorm a number of alternatives. The team could come up with twenty or thirty suggestions to solve the problem of too many accidents. Evaluating and choosing among so many alternatives would be difficult.

The first step the team would take would be to group any similar suggestions and possibly eliminate those that, on further scrutiny, may not have enough merit. From there, the team leader would help the team decide on the five or six top alternatives. Each team member would anonymously rank order each of the alternatives on a piece of paper. A recorder would then review each team member's choices and record the rankings, as in the example in figure 26.

Decision-Making Using Nominal Group Technique

Team Members' Rankings

Alternatives for Reducing Accidents in the Workplace	#1	#2	#3	#4	#5	#6	Raw Score	Rank Order
1. Non-skid ramps	5	3	3	3	5	4	23	4
2. Regular safety training	1	2	1	1	4	1	10	1
3. Improved lighting throughout the facility	2	4	2	2	3	3	16	2
4. Upgrade equipment	3	5	6	4	2	6	26	5
5. Safety shoes	6	6	5	5	6	5	33	6
6. Move boxes and clutter to inventory area and keep them there	4	1	4	6	1	2	18	3

Fig. 26. The Nominal Group Technique can be effectively used by teams to make decisions.

To achieve the raw score, add across horizontally for each item. Then rank the alternatives from low raw score to high raw score.

> *"I learned during my years out of coaching that, regardless of what business you're in, you're going to have problems. How you deal with them is what counts. You don't turn your back on them."*
>
> —Dan Reeves, Football Coach

In this example, the best alternative for minimizing accidents would be *regular safety training*. If there is enough money in the budget to process additional alternatives, the next suggestion would be to improve the lighting throughout the facility.

While teams probably can't use nominal group technique to solve every problem, it can be helpful when time is of the essence. It works best when the team size isn't too large, preferably no more than about eleven people.

Synergy and Creativity in Problem Solving

For teams to effectively solve problems and make decisions, the team leader must influence a climate of creativity and cooperation. Remember, people have a tendency to compete against each other. In the problem-solving process, competition among team members to get their ideas implemented can cause the entire process to stall.

The team leader needs to monitor team discussions and help team members move beyond conflict. By continually encouraging team members to stay focused on the problem rather than on competing with each other, the emphasis is more likely to be on creative solutions.

As team members present ideas, they will likely trigger creative ideas in others. This creative team atmosphere leads to more alternatives and, thus, better solutions to problems. This type of interaction among team members is called *synergy*. The sum of the parts is greater than the individual effect. In other words, two heads are better than one!

"None of us is as smart as all of us."

—Roy Disney

Here are some key reminders for establishing a creative, synergistic climate:

- **Encourage brainstorming.** Get ideas out on the table.
- **Encourage open communication.** Create an environment in which ideas are welcomed without fear of reprisal.
- **Encourage self-disclosure.** Reward team members for sharing their ideas. Sometimes people don't want to disclose their ideas because they feel that retaining them puts them in a superior position. This is a form of competition.
- **Never put ideas down.** Keep an open mind to all possibilities. Through deductive reasoning, the team will likely close in on the best ideas to solve problems.
- **Write ideas down.** While the team is "synergizing," someone should be recording all ideas. Later, the team can select the best ideas and use nominal group technique or deductive reasoning to choose the best idea.
- **Don't get "bogged down" in philosophy.** Some problem-solving sessions can become a quagmire of hyperbole. In other words, people may talk and talk and talk to support their idea rather than noting the idea and moving on. Discussion of the best ideas comes later.

> *"What sustains a company is the recognition that service and innovation are built on a bedrock of listening, trust, and respect for the creative potential of each employee."*
> —Tom Peters and Nancy Austin, *A Passion for Excellence*

- **Make the environment creative.** Be aware of the meeting room and site. Be sure that the audiovisual tools for visual learning are available. Occasionally, hold retreats so the team can get away from a familiar environment. Often a new setting sparks creativity.
- **Have fun.** A sense of humor takes the edge off the decision-making process and helps people stay loose.

Thinking Beyond the Ordinary

People are often encouraged to think conventionally rather than creatively. From childhood they are told to "stay within the lines." Such admonishments can stifle creativity.

The trend continues in the workplace, where creativity is often discouraged rather than encouraged. People learn that new and different ideas are odd and so are the people who present them. They learn to go along with conventional wisdom.

Following are two common exercises to test your creativity. Take a few minutes to respond to each.

"When you have to make a choice and don't make it, that is in itself a choice."

—William James

The Nine-Dot Exercise

Connect the dots below by using no more than four straight lines. The lines cannot be retraced, and you may not lift your writing instrument from the paper.

O   O   O

O   O   O

O   O   O

"Men go abroad to wonder at the heights of mountains, at the huge waves of the sea, at the long courses of the rivers, at the vast compass of the ocean, at the circular motions of the stars; and they pass by themselves without wondering."

—St. Augustine (Take the time to consider what might be)

The Dot-in-the-Circle Exercise

Draw the illustration below on a separate piece of paper without lifting your writing instrument from the paper.

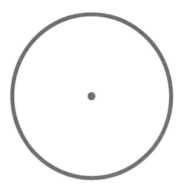

Turn to page 198 to see the answers.

Again, the emphasis is on thinking beyond the conventional. If you tried to solve this problem thinking only within the circle, you couldn't arrive at an answer.

What's the lesson of these two exercises?

Look beyond the obvious. Think beyond the conventional boundaries.

Let your creativity flow.

The Four Major Team Climates

In figure 27, the seven-step, rational problem-solving process overlays a "creative solutions" model. The model helps define the various climates or cultures that can exist in a team environment. Of course, what your team should strive for is the upper righthand quadrant: AGIWTHC—a great idea whose time has come.

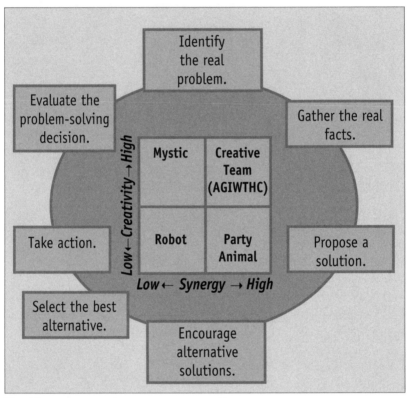

Fig. 27. *Creativity Plus Synergy = AGIWTHC.*

Quadrant 1: The Robot (low creativity, low synergy). The team leader solves all problems and makes all decisions. The team is expected to do what it is told. Team members act like robots. They don't think for themselves, and creativity and brainstorming are discouraged.

Quadrant 2: The Mystic (high creativity, low synergy). Here, team members may be creative as individuals but they don't share or disclose information, knowledge, and ideas. In other words, team members may frequently "go to the mountain top." They seriously contemplate problems and potential solutions, but they don't put their heads together or synergize. Thus, they aren't in a position to build on ideas and potential solutions. The team leader doesn't encourage team members to communicate with each other.

Quadrant 3: The Party Animal (high synergy, low creativity). Team members communicate with each other, but there is no serious follow through on suggested solutions to problems. They don't build on ideas. Ideas and potential solutions aren't written down and acted on. The team has fun, but nothing gets done. Problems aren't solved and decisions aren't made.

Quadrant 4: The Creative Team (high creativity, high synergy). The team leader encourages team members to openly discuss problems and build on suggested alternatives. Everyone is encouraged to participate and to listen to the creative ideas of other team members. The team focuses on effective problem solving and decision making. They continuously look for AGIWTHC.

What's Your Problem-Solving Style?

Team members solve problems in different ways. Some are more reflective. Some are quick decision makers. Some want to gather all the facts before they will act. Below is a survey to help you understand your problem-solving style. Your whole team may want to take the survey.

An Informal Preference Survey

Instructions: Below are five sets of words or phrases. Considering the first thing that comes to mind, rank the items in each set from 1 through 4 (1=most preferred, 4=least preferred). In each set, be sure to write a different number next to each item. There are no right or wrong, better or worse answers.

1. A team member informs me of a dispute regarding other members' deadlines. As a team leader, the first things I consider in solving a problem are:

   a _____ The perspective of those involved.

   b _____ The perspective of experts.

   c _____ Relevant facts and data.

   d _____ My own experience.

2. In the past, I've handled problems by:

   a _____ Reviewing past history.

   b _____ Collecting facts/data/evidence.

   c _____ Trial and error.

   d _____ Discussing the situation with other people.

3. I've found that the best team results come from:

a _____ Open discussion.

b _____ Inviting increased competition.

c _____ Persuading.

d _____ Informing.

4. My idea of effective problem solving is:

a _____ Taking decisive action.

b _____ Reviewing and considering alternatives.

c _____ Assembling complete data and facts.

d _____ Investigating the causes.

5. Which of the following best sums up your philosophy about problem solving?

a _____ "To be successful, a solution needs to be collaborative."

b _____ "Past experience is the best teacher."

c _____ "Solving problems comes from getting to the root cause."

d _____ "Sometimes you just have to act, without knowing fully the cause of the problem."

"You miss 100 percent of the shots you never take."
—Wayne Gretzky

Scoring Instructions: Each item in each of the five sets corresponds to one of four problem-solving styles. To score the survey, write your numerical rankings in the appropriate spaces below. Then total the numbers in each column.

1a _____   1b _____   1c_____   1d _____

2d _____   2a _____   2b _____   2c _____

3c _____   3d _____   3a _____   3b _____

4b _____   4c _____   4d _____   4a _____

5a _____   5b _____   5c_____   5d _____

Total _____ (A) Total_____ (T) Total _____ (I) Total_____ (C)

Four Problem-Solving Styles

The labels *Ambassador, Thinker, Investigator,* and *Charger* describe four typical problem-solving styles. Your lowest score on the survey indicates your preferred style. The second lowest score indicates your "back-up" style. Each of us has some of the traits of each style, although one style usually predominates. This survey is designed to help you recognize the strengths and avoid the pitfalls of your preferred style.

Ambassador (A)

- Strives for mutual agreement
- Listens to and values ideas and opinions of other team members
- Zeroes in on logical and practical solutions
- Easily influences other team members
- Tends to conform to prevailing group ideas and thoughts
- Sometimes adopts stopgap solutions rather than focusing on long-range solutions

Thinker (T)

- Studies framework of ideas
- Researches history of problems and solutions that have been tried before
- Analyzes similar situations to derive an answer to problems
- Views issues in "black-and-white," without emotional attachment
- Tends to be indecisive when faced wtih several possible solutions

Investigator (I)

- Wants to identify the source of the problem(s).
- Looks only for facts directly related to problem
- Favors first-hand information and personally observing the situation
- Very methodical in decision making
- Defines circumstances to get a better understanding of what caused situation at hand
- Often perceived as lacking people skills

Charger (C)

- Occupied with the outcome
- Likes to test theories before making a decision
- Maintains a do-it-yourself attitude
- Values intuition
- Keeps a level head during stressful situations
- Tends to make on-the-spot decisions; sometimes perceived as disagreeable and uncompromising

Answers to Exercises, p.190-191

The Nine-Dot Exercise

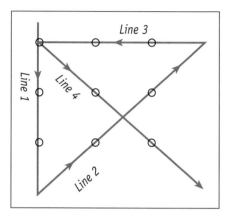

You have to go beyond the traditional bounds to complete this exercise. The dotted lines represent how many people tend to think. They will try to solve the problem within the box, within the traditional parameters. As the illustration indicates, team members must think beyond the boundaries of the box to come up with the solution.

The Dot-in-the-Circle Exercise

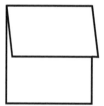 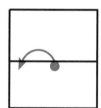 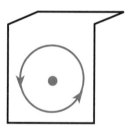

Step 1: Fold the upper third of your paper into a one-third section so that it folds across the front of the paper.

Step 2: Draw a dot just below the fold part of the paper. Drag a line from the dot across the fold.

Step 3: Release the fold so that the whole paper is flat on your writing surface. Then complete the exercise by drawing a circle.

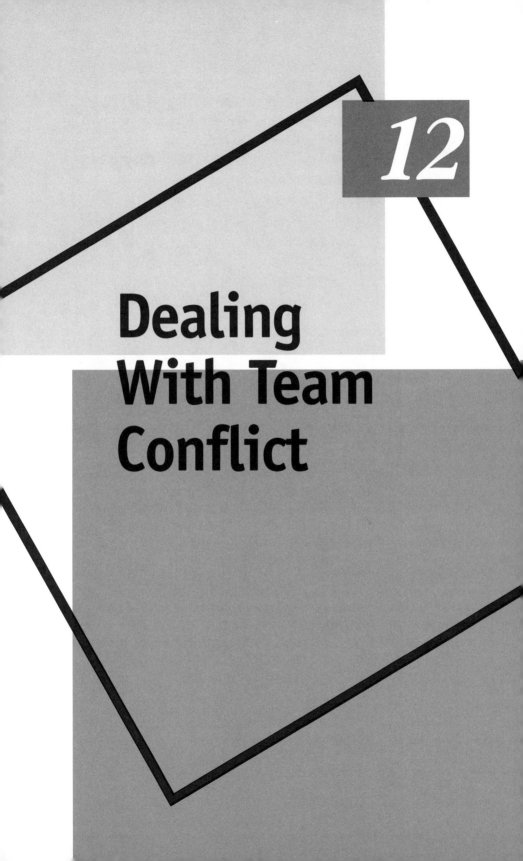

12

Dealing With Team Conflict

There's a story told of a swami and a cobra who lived near a temple in Bengal. As people went to worship, the cobra would bite them; many became fearful and refused to visit the temple. The swami, who was the master of the temple, summoned the cobra to him and, by means of a spell, made the snake promise he would never bite anyone again.

Soon it became known that the snake had lost its venom and was no longer a threat. People grew unafraid of the cobra, and boys began to tease the snake unmercifully. They hit it and dragged it over the stones.

One day the temple swami summoned the snake to see if he had kept his promise. The cobra was bruised and bleeding.

"How did this come to be?" asked the swami.

"I have been abused," said the snake, "ever since you condemned me to my promise."

"I told you not to bite," said the swami, "but I did not tell you not to hiss."

Moral of the story: It's okay to disagree. It's just not okay to be disagreeable. Conflict is necessary to arrive at better solutions. It's not *who* has the best solution that is important, but rather finding the solution that will benefit the team and the customer best.

Defining Conflict

Conflict is good!

Yes, that's right. Conflict means that team members are sharing ideas. However, their ideas may be contrary to each other. Thus, team members disagree. Disagreement is healthy, as long as team members keep talking and listening. Too often when there is disagreement, people stop listening to each other. They may assume that they're right and the other person is wrong. That's when conflict becomes unhealthy.

Conflict management is the idea of confronting the differences and disagreements, staying focused on resolving the conflict, and arriving at acceptable conclusions to solve problems, make decisions, and carry out goals.

Let's look at several definitions of conflict:

1. **Conflict is an expressed struggle between two interdependent parties who perceive incompatible goals, scarce rewards or resources, and interference from the other party in achieving goals, priorities, and tasks.** This means that each party involved perceives the other parties as trying to block the achievement of goals and tasks. The feeling is that others are intentionally stifling achievement. The aggrieved party will often fight back, escalating the conflict.

2. **Conflict is the dynamic tension between people who are different.** Dynamic tension means that each party is passionately committed to his or her point of view. When the other person is in disagreement, the aggrieved party sometimes considers the other person to be difficult. Usually, however, the other person just has a different, impassioned viewpoint.

3. **Conflict is the difference between expectations and reality.** The people involved in the conflict have different perceptions about the facts of a situation. They may each have a different concept of a goal that is supposed to be achieved, how to accomplish it, when to do it, and who is supposed to do what. With the distortion of facts comes different expectations. When one party doesn't live up to the other party's perceived expectations, there is often conflict. For example, if five team members are in a meeting in which the team leader suggests a goal and method for accomplishing it, each team member might hear a different message. As a result, they each do something different. If they fail in achieving the goal, it's very possible that they'll blame each other because they had different expectations

Causes of Team Conflict

Conflict may occur on several levels. At each successive level, it becomes more difficult to resolve.

Level 1 Conflicts: Disagreement on facts and data. This level is often called "the fact difference." Quite simply, team members have different perceptions of the facts. Team members jump to conclusions and become emotionally involved instead of asking for more facts. Many conflicts can be resolved if team members will just share their facts, and if others will genuinely listen to the facts.

Level 2 Conflicts: Disagreement about methodology. Team members disagree on how to do the work. It is the "my idea is better than your idea" mind-set. Team members compete against each other rather than strive for a common method of carrying out the work. Sometimes, team members can agree to use different methods as long as they achieve the intended results.

Level 3 Conflicts: Disagreement on goals. At this level of conflict, team members disagree about what to do. This type of conflict immobilizes teams. Team members become frustrated because they keep arguing and aren't accomplishing anything. The team members sometimes give up on goals and focus on the routine work to avoid dealing with conflict. The team leader must be diligent in keeping the team focused on setting goals.

> *"The best index to a person's character is how he treats people who can't do him any good, and how he treats people who can't fight back."*
>
> —Abigail VanBuren

Level 4 Conflicts: Disagreement about priorities. At this level of conflict, team members can't decide on the priorities—either among themselves or even with the team leader. Yet another area of conflict involves a team leader or an upper manager who continually changes the priorities. Team members don't know what to work on, and frustration develops. As discussed earlier, two factors should help determine team priorities: (1) perceived payoff of the goal or task and (2) deadlines. A goal or activity that has an immediate deadline is likely a higher priority right now than one that has a deadline of next year.

Level 5 Conflicts: Different values. Values conflicts are very difficult to resolve. Team members grow up with different values. They attended different schools, had different parents, and grew up in different neighborhoods, different parts of the country, or even different countries. A team leader can't expect that a group of people with different backgrounds will always agree with each other. Team leaders should continually work to help team members stay focused on what they can agree on rather than allow them to become polarized.

"People with tact have less to retract."
—Arnold H. Glasow

Confrontation Styles

Confrontation is often viewed as a negative behavior because often during confrontations people become combative and competitive. But if team members stay focused on the problem, they confront the problem. The key, then, in conflict resolution is to confront the problem, not the person. The accompanying chart offers a comparison of various confrontation styles.

Five Conflict Resolution Styles

Style	Confrontive Behavior	Outcome
Avoidance	Team members avoid discussing issues because it is uncomfortable. They hope the conflict will go away. Team members choose not to confront the problem.	LOSE-LOSE. Everyone loses because the team members are evasive. There is no attempt to solve the problem. They are neither assertive nor cooperative.
Competition	Team members compete against each other for who has the best solution for solving problems. Team members confront each other rather than the problem.	WIN-LOSE. Team members try to win and cause the other person to lose. Team members are aggressive and uncooperative. They prefer to overpower with their point of view rather than to listen to others' viewpoints.

Style	Confrontive Behavior	Outcome
Accommodation	Team members accommodate each other, but they may not be assertive in explaining and negotiating for their point of view. Their goal is to be liked rather than respected. They would rather cooperate than run the risk of being perceived as disagreeable. They just go along.	LOSE-WIN. Team members are not assertive in expressing their ideas. Instead, they cooperate to avoid conflict. They "go along" even if they disagree. Very seldom is the best solution to a problem emphasized in this scenario. Instead, safe decisions are made.
Collaboration	Team members confront problems to find the best solution. The emphasis is on creative solutions. Ideas are encouraged and listened to. The team collaborates to decide on the best solution.	WIN-WIN. Team members are both cooperative and assertive. They listen to the ideas of others and assume responsibility for presenting new ideas for consideration.
Compromise	Team members confront problems, but may not be able to collaboratively decide on the best solution. Each party is willing to give something up to achieve a cooperative agreement. Thus, they compromise since they can't reach agreement on any one idea.	WIN-WIN. Team members are very cooperative. They are assertive in presenting potential solutions, but realize they must back off when others aren't convinced that the solution will solve the problem. So the team looks at parts of several solutions to settle for one they can live with. Better decisions are made, increasing the likelihood that the whole team will win.

The main point of all this? The team should always strive for a win-win solution to team problems.

Practical Tips for Resolving Team Conflicts

1. **Listen. Don't interrupt. Try to understand the other team member's point of view.** Only after you have listened for understanding should you attempt to respond. Interrupting others while they are speaking not only shows disrespect, it keeps you from understanding the other person's perspective.

2. **Accept the right of another team member to disagree or have a different opinion.** Remember, everyone has different experiences and values. Don't compete against others to prove that you are right and they are wrong. Simply acknowledge their point of view. It doesn't mean you agree or disagree.

3. **State your opinions and feelings directly but calmly.** Be succinct. Concentrate on communicating clearly and concisely. Make your point and stop talking. It bores others when people ramble on and hog the conversation. Be assertive, but don't be aggressive. Assertive communication states a viewpoint. Aggressive communication forces a viewpoint.

4. **Don't start the conversation with your mind made up.** Be willing to let other team members contribute to your ideas. Be open-minded enough to build on those ideas.

5. **Don't compete and try to win all the time at the expense of others.** Instead, realize that others want to have their ideas accepted and that they want to win too. Concentrate on compromise and/or collaboration to create win-win solutions.

6. **Stick to the present—not the past.** Sometimes during disagreements, team members bring up the past mistakes of those they disagree with or use excuses to reject others' ideas. They may make statements like "We tried that before" or "It didn't work the last time we tried it." While it's always

important to learn from the past, it shouldn't be used as a weapon against present ideas or as an indicator that your present idea will fail.

7. **Raise the level of discussion.** Concentrate on what you can agree on rather than on what you disagree on. Identify and stay focused on the higher purpose to which each team member is committed.

8. **Use a rational, objective method to solve the problem.** As suggested in reference to the rational problem-solving process, identify the real problem. The team needs to seek out the facts related to the conflict rather than just deal with surface-level issues. A lack of facts leads to emotions, which usually escalates conflict. Deescalate conflict by modeling rational behavior.

9. **Take a break.** If team members become too emotional or if they reach an impasse, call for a time out. Give everyone an opportunity to cool off and to come back to the table with a fresh perspective. Often, when team members are in disagreement, polarization occurs. Each party becomes more fervent in his or her viewpoint. Taking a break can help team members rethink their position and help them see others' perspectives.

10. **Enjoy the rewards when you reach agreement.** Striving for agreement is a sign your team is maturing. Team members are cooperating with each other instead of competing with each other. That's worth rejoicing about.

"An optimist may see a light where there is none, but why must the pessimist always run to blow it out?"

—Michel de Saint-Pierre

13

Conducting Effective Team Meetings

> *"No more good must be attempted than the people can bear."*
>
> —Thomas Jefferson (Keep meetings brief and to the point.)

Purposes of Team Meetings

Teams hold meetings usually for one of three purposes:

1. To solve problems related to goods, services, or procedures that affect customers

2. To make effective decisions so that action can begin

3. To share information that keeps team members informed and assists them in problem solving and decision making

Team meetings that stay focused on these purposes usually have productive outcomes. Although both the team leader and the team members share responsibility for making meetings useful, focused, and productive, team leaders should set the tone.

Obstacles to Effective Meetings

One of the ways team leaders set the tone is to remove obstacles to productive meetings. Several common obstacles and how to prevent or minimize them follow:

- **No agenda.** Lack of an agenda is probably the biggest obstacle to conducting effective meetings. If there is no agenda, what will team members talk about? The answer: Anything and everything. The team leader and/or meeting organizer should coordinate the meeting agenda with feedback from team members.

- **No time limits.** Meetings usually have a designated starting time, but not an ending time. If there is no ending time indicated, when will meetings end? The answer: Who knows? Fortunately, lunch time or going home time intervenes.

Remember Parkinson's Law: Work expands to fill the time that's available. If the time available is indefinite, then the work will likely continue to expand.

- **Lack of leadership.** One of the most frustrating meeting obstacles is lack of effective leadership to guide and direct meetings. The formal leader and the informal leaders help keep meeting agenda items focused, ensure they are communicated effectively, facilitate discussion of agenda items, and bring them to closure. The team then makes a decision, solves a problem, and effectively communicates and shares information.

- **Little or no participation.** Team members are discouraged from participating because they are put down when they do, fear taking responsibility, or fear their input may be wrong. Effective decisions can't be made and problems can't be meaningfully solved unless team members share their perspectives. Everyone on the team must be encouraged to participate.

- **Domination.** This occurs when one or a few team members dominate discussions and endlessly elaborate. Such behavior discourages others from participating, and they quit paying attention to what's being discussed. Some team members can be intimidated by more boisterous, aggressive meeting attendees.

- **Frequent digressions.** One huge obstacle to solving problems and making decisions occurs when team members stray off the topic. One subject leads to another and another and sometimes the group never returns to the original topic. Team

Two managers talking: "Let's cut the staff meeting today." "We can't. I need the sleep."

—Joe Griffith

members leave the meeting frustrated because nothing is resolved. In fact, digressing from the topic can lead to many different discussions and, therefore, more unresolved issues. It's important for the team leader to keep the team on the subject.

- **The wrong people.** People are often invited to meetings as a courtesy rather than for what they can contribute. The wrong people either contribute nothing because they don't know why they're at the meeting or they contribute information that may be irrelevant since they're not familiar with the issues.

- **Frequent interruptions.** In some meetings, everyone wants to talk and no one wants to listen. Team members may frequently be interrupted, keeping them from making their key points. These interruptions also affect the flow of the meeting and can lead to frequent digressions. People who are frequently interrupted may become defensive, causing conflict.

- **No summary or follow up.** A meeting is not successful unless action gets taken on the decisions that are made. After a meeting is over, no one will know who is to do what if decisions aren't noted, certain team members aren't charged with responsibility for carrying out the decision, and team members aren't held accountable for follow up. Meetings should always have some kind of resulting action. These actions and who is accountable for them need to be summarized and immediately distributed to team members.

- **Lack of preparation.** It is difficult to discuss issues, share information, make decisions, and solve problems if team members are unprepared. What contributes to this problem is

"A meeting is no substitute for progress."
—Author Unknown

that team members often don't receive an agenda or information about agenda items to study before the meeting. Often, the information is handed out as the meeting is being held. The team members try to read about the issues and listen at the same time. Often, ill-advised decisions are made since team members don't have the time to prepare.

- **Lengthy, boring presentations.** Sometimes these types of presentations occur because the speaker hasn't adequately prepared. Or people who don't know what they want to say often just start talking. Or a presenter's selfish passion for the subject can contribute to the problem. The speaker may not realize that other team members don't share the same interest in the subject. Team leaders should make sure presenters have adequate time to prepare and encourage presentations to be short and to the point.

- **Unresolved conflicts.** Yet another major obstacle to effective meetings are team members who compete with each other for who has the best ideas. To make decisions and solve problems, team members must focus on compromise and collaboration. Continuous conflict without resolution can cause a team to disintegrate.

- **Negative attitudes.** Attitude becomes an obstacle when the team focuses on what can't be done instead of what *can* be accomplished. Here, when issues are discussed and potential solutions are offered, some team members say things like "we've tried it before" or "it doesn't work." There's a big difference between being negative and being constructive and between disagreeing and being disagreeable. Stay focused on the positive.

There's a story about a positive little boy and a negative little boy. The negative young man is put into a room filled with shiny toys. The positive boy is put into a room filled with horse manure.

A psychologist who is studying the two boys observes the negative little boy sitting among all the toys and complaining. "There are too many toys in here. I don't know which ones to play with. I'm bored. I wish they'd let me go home," says the negative little boy.

The psychologist next observes the positive little boy shoveling horse manure furiously, with a smile on his face. Curious, the psychologist opens the doors and asks the positive boy what he's doing. The young man replies, "I know there's a pony in here somewhere!"

The moral of the story? There's a lot of manure out there. Stay focused on the ponies. Think positive, not negative!

Planning for Team Meetings With an Extended Agenda

An extended agenda is a planning tool that can be used to carry out effective meetings. It can also be used as the actual agenda at a meeting. Here are some of the primary elements of an extended agenda (they're also illustrated in fig. 28):

- **The primary purpose of the meeting.** If a primary purpose can't be defined, then the meeting should be canceled.
- **Agenda items that are relevant to the meeting's purpose.** Agenda items shouldn't be created just so the team can have a meeting.
- **A definite start and end time.** The cumulative time allotments for each agenda item helps you determine the length of the meetings. Always start and end on time.

- **The internal or external customer who benefits by your discussion.** Keep the customer informed.
- **Who will lead the discussion for each agenda item.** A discussion about what is to be discussed and how much time to devote to the discussion should be held between the team leader or meeting planner and the team member who will present the item.
- **The potential outcome.** A meeting agenda item usually has one or a combination of these three outcomes:

  1. To make a decision

  2. To solve a problem

  3. To share information

  At the end of the discussion of an agenda item, always ask whether the intended outcome was achieved.

- **The handouts to support agenda items.** These handouts should always be shared with team members in advance of the meeting, preferably at least seventy-two hours before. This gives team members the opportunity to review and prepare. They can attend the meeting ready to give input, make decisions, and solve problems.

Agenda

Purpose of meeting: To make a decision on the budget for the building refurbishing project

Time: 9:00 a.m.-11:00 a.m.

Agenda Item	Time Allotment	Presenter	Client/ Customer	Intended Response/ Outcome	Handouts
Status of inventory control project	30 minutes 9:00 a.m.- 9:30 a.m.	Paul Heacock	Frontline sales reps	Information sharing/ problem solving	Proposed re-engineering of inventory processing
Discussion and evaluation of new budgeting software	40 minutes 9:30 a.m.- 10:10 a.m.	Dale Hotze	Finance department team	Information sharing/ decision making	List of features, benefits, possible drawbacks to software
Review and discussion of building refurbishing project budget	35 minutes 10:10 a.m.- 10:45 a.m.	Tammy Schuman	All office staff	Decision making	Budget proposal to refurbish building
Update on new market research	15 minutes 10:45 a.m.- 11:00 a.m.	Marcella Smith	The whole team	Information sharing	None

Fig. 28. *The extended agenda is a tool for conducting successful meetings.*

The sample of an extended agenda in figure 29 has been designed as a model for you to use as you plan your team meetings. The Meeting Summary Form in figure 30 can be used to report important actions and accountabilities so proper follow up is more likely to occur.

SAMPLE
Extended Meeting Agenda

Team Name _____

Meeting Date _____

Meeting Facilitator _____

Purpose of meeting: _____

Begins at: _____ Ends at: _____

Agenda Item	Time Allotment	Presenter	Client/ Customer	Intended Response/ Outcome	Handouts

Fig. 29. *Sample extended meeting agenda.*

SAMPLE
Meeting Summary

Team Name _____

Date of Meeting _____

Today's Date _____

Important Actions:

1. Agenda Item: _____

   _____

   Outcome: _____

   _____

   Follow up (Who will do what): _____

   _____

   _____

2. Agenda Item: _____

   _____

   Outcome: _____

   _____

   Follow up (Who will do what): _____

   _____

   _____

3. Agenda Item: _____

   _____

   Outcome: _____

   _____

   Follow up (Who will do what): _____

   _____

   _____

Fig. 30. *Sample Meeting Summary form.*

More Ideas for Keeping Team Meetings on Track

- **Appoint a task master/time keeper.** This person has the authority and responsibility to interrupt at any time. If the discussion about an agenda item begins to digress, the task master can speak up and remind team members of their need to stay focused on the task. This person can also inform the team when it is spending too much time on an agenda item straying from the schedule. A different taskmaster/time keeper should be selected at each meeting so all team members have an opportunity to play this role.

- **Appoint a recorder.** A meeting recorder stands at a flipchart during the meeting and records the *important actions* of the meeting, the decisions that are made and the problems that are solved. The recorder also lists the *accountabilities*, who volunteered or who was asked to carry out an assignment or task. Again, this position should be rotated so that all team members eventually serve as the recorder.

- **Use the "100 mile" rule.** The team should act as though any meeting is one hundred miles from the nearest phone and other interruptions. When teams are trying to discuss important issues, it's very disruptive for members to be called out of the meeting to take phone calls or deal with other interruptions. It interferes with the flow of the meeting and adversely affects decision making and problem solving.

- **Penalize lateness.** Don't go back and summarize for latecomers. That rewards them for being late. Also, if the team can agree, develop some kind of a "fine" for latecomers. For example, for every minute team members are late, they are fined a nickel. The money can be used for coffee, other refreshments, or as a contribution to a team party.

- **Pay attention to aesthetics.** Make it comfortable for team members to participate. For most team meetings, a round table arrangement is usually best. Team members can see each other better and can make eye contact. As one team member is presenting, everyone is included in the discussion.

  Also pay attention to the lighting and temperature control. Both affect whether team members will participate or become lethargic.

- **Use visuals.** A picture is worth a thousand words. Many people learn visually. Charts and graphs can be wonderful tools for illustrating or summarizing data. Using an overhead projector or flip chart to display ideas gives everyone an overview of the discussion. And, if your budget allows, sophisticated software is available for developing presentations.

- **Help people prepare for their presentations.** Team leaders should inform team members *before* meetings if they are going to be called on to speak. The extended agenda can remind the team leader or meeting planner to ask or inform team members to be prepared prior to the meeting. One of the biggest meeting time wasters is asking team members to speak on issues they haven't had any opportunity to prepare for.

"Business meetings are important. One reason is that they demonstrate how many people the company can operate without."

—Anonymous

- **Summarize each discussion point.** Miscommunication is another big problem in meetings. Team members filter information in different ways. Before moving on to the next issue, the discussion of the current agenda item should always be summarized. You can do this by asking for feedback and asking clarifying questions.

- **Have fun!** Humor breaks tension. It can also help team members be more creative and not take themselves or the issues too seriously. It helps them to keep problems and concerns in perspective. If team members learn to have fun, they are more likely to get down to business when they need to.

"Nothing more effectively involves people, sustains credibility, or generates enthusiasm than face-to-face communication. It is critical to provide and discuss all organization performance figures with all of our people.

—Dana Corporation Philosophy

Checklist for Planning and Running Effective Team Meetings

Before the meeting:

☐ Circulate a meaningful agenda.

☐ Make sure the right people are asked to attend.

☐ Remind team members often about the meeting and its purpose.

☐ Get into the habit of asking "Can we do this without a meeting?

At the meeting:

☐ Start on time; don't recap the discussion for late arrivals.

☐ Open with a brief review of team goals to remind the team of its overall purpose.

☐ Briefly review the primary purpose and the agenda.

☐ Stick to the agenda. Resist the tendency to stray.

☐ Appoint a "taskmaster/timekeeper" to keep the meeting moving.

☐ Appoint a "recorder" to keep team members focused on what's been discussed and decided.

☐ Use handouts and audiovisuals when they can support agenda items.

☐ List accurately the actions and accountabilities decided at the meeting.

☐ Summarize the discussion.

☐ Thank team members for their preparation and feedback.

After the meeting:

☐ Distribute an action-oriented summary within 24 to 48 hours.

☐ Be sure any follow-up meetings are scheduled.

☐ Evaluate the last meeting: "What can we do to improve?"

☐ Celebrate successes!

Exercise:

Team Meeting Effectiveness Evaluation

Directions: Each team member and the team leader should anonymously complete the evaluation below. It is best to fill it out during or right after a team meeting so the responses are timely and spontaneous. Complete the evaluation at least biannually to give your team feedback about the strengths and weaknesses of its meetings. Circle the number you feel most closely corresponds with your feelings, with "1" meaning you strongly disagree and "5" indicating you strongly agree.

1. The purpose of our team meetings is well-defined.   1 2 3 4 5

2. An agenda is circulated at least 72 hours before the meetings.   1 2 3 4 5

3. Handouts related to agenda items are circulated at least 72 hours before the meeting.   1 2 3 4 5

4. Team meetings start and end on time.   1 2 3 4 5

5. Participation by team members is strongly encouraged.   1 2 3 4 5

6. Team members voluntarily present ideas and disclose information that can help the team solve problems and make decisions.   1 2 3 4 5

7. There is broad participation in discussion rather than a few team members dominating discussion.   1 2 3 4 5

8. The team stays focused on the discussion at hand rather than digressing to other subjects.　　1　2　3　4　5

9. Team meetings have few interruptions.　1　2　3　4　5

10. The team leader or other team members routinely summarize discussion at the conclusion of an agenda topic.　　1　2　3　4　5

11. The team allocates the meeting time well for each agenda item.　　1　2　3　4　5

12. The team leader and team members arrive at meetings well prepared.　　1　2　3　4　5

13. Lengthy, boring presentations are kept to a minimum.　　1　2　3　4　5

14. The team effectively resolves conflicts in a timely manner.　　1　2　3　4　5

15. Negative attitudes are dealt with quickly and are not a major problem.　　1　2　3　4　5

16. The meeting room is prepared for audiovisual needs.　　1　2　3　4　5

17. The meeting room is comfortable, with adequate lighting and temperature control.　　1　2　3　4　5

18. Side chatter and unsolicited small group discussions are controlled.　　1　2　3　4　5

19. A meeting summary of important actions and accountabilities is distributed to team members within 48 hours of the meeting.　　1　2　3　4　5

20. The team has fun!　　1　2　3　4　5

Total (add your total points) _____

81-100	The team likely has excellent, productive meetings.
61-80	The team has good meetings, but needs to focus a little more on a few key areas.
41-60	The team likely has a difficult time getting through and following up on meetings. The team leader and selected team members need to brainstorm and make recommendations for improvement.
40 or below	Team meetings are probably ineffective. Problems aren't being solved and decisions aren't being made. The team leader and selected team members need to start now to make recommendations for overhauling team meetings.

"The achievements of an organization are the result of the combined efforts of each individual."
—Vince Lombardi

14

Staying the Course

> *More races are won through patience and attrition than any other factors.*
>
> —Richard Petty, race car driver

Team Building: A Real Commitment

One of the big myths in team building is that a team can be developed just because the company or organization has decided to form one. As this book has discussed, teams need to be nurtured, encouraged, focused, and properly directed. Teams don't just happen. There must be a true commitment to team building from the top down.

A "cheerleading" speech by the chief executive or another manager assailing the attributes of a team won't make it happen. Managers who espouse team building need to model the behaviors they want their employees to have. Team members must to be praised and rewarded for exhibiting team-building behaviors.

Staying the course means that the commitment to team building is strong enough to overcome the adversities related to team building. Often managers and team members give up when the going gets tough, saying to others in the organization that "this team building stuff just doesn't work."

It works! But you must get past the hurdles. Team building is a long-term process that requires an overall organizational behavior change. Managers must gradually make the transition from using power over people to empowering people. Team members must gradually learn to accept authority and responsibility.

Myths About the Team-Building Process

Most of this book has focused on the actions that can be taken at the team level to make a team successful. However, there are organizational obstacles that prevent a team from achieving its goals. Here are a few common organizational misconceptions about teams:

- **Teams are natural. Almost everyone has participated on some kind of team.** While sports teams, debate teams, and other kinds of teams share some similarities to work teams, they also share differences. Being on a team isn't just "natural." Team members must work at cooperating rather than competing, sharing rather than withholding, and striving for team success rather than personal gain. Team building requires hard work and diligence. It isn't natural.

- **Any group can be turned into a team.** Not true. Sometimes management tries to force team building. Some work groups and work situations just aren't conducive to team building. Sometimes the personality make-up of the employees discourages team building. The nature of the work processes may be inhibiting. While most employee work situations encourage team building, be aware that team building isn't right for every situation.

- **Changing from a traditional hierarchical organization to a team organization is easily and quickly achieved.** As discussed in this book, a team must go through a socialization process. At each stage of team development, team members' behavior changes. The organization must undergo a similar change. And just as this process takes time for a team, it does for the organization as well. Be wary of the upper management mandate that says: "We will have teams firmly in place within the next six months. That's an order."

- **Teams should strive to become "self-directed" as quickly as possible.** "Self-directed work teams" is a buzz phrase. Some organizations try to transition directly into self-directed work teams. Management abdicates authority and responsibility to team members immediately. The transfer of power is sudden and chaotic. Team members become confused and bewildered. They resist the power they've been given. In this scenario, upper management ends up saying, "Self-directed work teams don't work." What they fail to realize is that self-directed work teams evolve. They can't be mandated.

A Template for Team Building

By now you understand that building and keeping teams requires persistence, determination, commitment, and strong direction. The following model will give you an outline to follow as you step through the team-building process. Keep in mind that this model is a guideline. Each team-building situation is as unique as the people involved.

"It takes two wings for a bird to fly."

—Jesse Jackson

A Model for Building Teams

Check off each item when completed.

☐ 1. Hold informal discussions between managers and employees about team building to ascertain and create interest.

☐ 2. Conduct introductory team-building training for interested parties, including all levels of management and key informal leaders among employees. The purpose of the training is for employees to understand what team building really entails. (Note: It is a *must* for upper management to attend and participate.)

☐ 3. Once everyone understands what team building really is, determine with key managers and employees the level of interest and commitment to pursue team building.

☐ 4. Appoint a team building coordinator with full and absolute commitment and support from upper management.

☐ 5. Develop a "steering team" to oversee the team-building process. The ideal size of the steering team is seven to eleven employees composed of a cross-section of the work force, both management and nonmanagement.

☐ 6. The steering team develops a plan for gradually forming teams. It sets specific goals: how many teams, when they will be formed, a budget for team building, and what kind of training will be provided.

☐ 7. The steering team conducts a training needs assessment to prepare to train new team members. (See the Training Needs Assessment Form on page 167.)

☐   8. Pilot teams are developed based on who has the most interest. Teams should preferably be voluntary. Seek out departments where there is already management and employee interest. Current managers should serve as team leaders. When teams mature, leadership can rotate.

☐   9. Select for success. Don't force people to participate. Go to those who are willing, interested, and enthused. Set team building up for success.

☐ 10. Go slow to go fast. Don't be in a hurry to see how many teams you can have. Set up teams that get quality results and receive rewards for success. Then other employees will likely want to form and be on teams.

☐ 11. Pilot teams receive initial training. Suggested subjects include team building, problem solving, effective communication, conflict management, and personality styles.

☐ 12. Pilot teams set at least one quality-oriented goal to meet an internal or external customer need: to improve a product or service or to change and improve a process or procedure.

☐ 13. Pilot teams develop strategic plans to carry out their goals.

☐ 14. Pilot teams implement their goals with guidance and direction from the team leader and upper management.

☐ 15. Accomplishments are magnified. The team celebrates it if it's successful in reaching its goals.

☐ 16. Recruit for new teams and give present teams new challenges.

Profile of a Winning Team

- Works toward common goals
- Strives for quality in everything it does
- Understands that people are different
- Strives for cooperation, not competition
- Builds trust relationships
- Embraces the diversity of its members
- Strives for continuous improvement
- Develops members' skills through effective training
- Creates a motivating team climate
- Uses its time and talents efficiently
- Empowers all team members
- Accepts and embraces responsibility
- Maintains a positive attitude
- Solves problems and makes decisions
- Uses resources wisely
- Continually builds morale
- Confronts and resolves conflicts in a timely way
- Holds well-planned, efficient team meetings
- Welcomes challenge and gets results
- Has open and useful communication
- Recognizes everyone for accomplishments
- Shares successes

"We never know how high we are till we are called to rise; and then, if we are true to plan, our statures touch the skies."

—Emily Dickinson

Bibliography
& Suggested
Reading

Chang, Richard. *Success Through Teamwork*. Irvine, CA: Richard Chang Associates, 1994.

Douglass, Merrill E. and Donna N. Douglass. *Time Management for Teams*. New York: AMACOM, 1992.

Fisher, Kimball, Steven Rayner, and William Belgard. *Tips for Teams*. New York: McGraw–Hill, 1995.

Gardenswartz, Lee, and Anita Rowe. *Diverse Teams at Work*. Chicago: Irwin Professional Publishing, 1994.

Grote, Dick. *Discipline Without Punishment*. New York: AMACOM, 1995.

Hartzler, Meg, and Jane E. Henry. *Team Fitness: A How-to Manual for Building a Winning Team*. Milwaukee: ASQC Quality Press, 1994.

Harshman, Carl L. And Steven L. Phillips. *Teaming Up*. San Diego: Pfeiffer and Co., 1994.

Hicks, Robert F. and Diane Bone. *Self-Managing Teams*. Los Altos, CA: Crisp Publications, 1990.

Katzenbach, Jon, and Douglas Smith. *The Wisdom of Teams*. Boston: Harvard Business School Press, 1993.

Knowles, Malcolm. *The Modern Practice of Adult Education*. Chicago: Follett, 1980.

Lundy, James L. *Teams: How to Develop Peak Performance Teams for World Class Results*. Chicago: The Dartnell Corporation, 1994.

Macklin, Deborah Harrington. *Keeping the Team Going*. New York: AMACOM, 1996.

Maddux, Robert. *Team Building: An Exercise in Leadership*. Los Altos, CA: Crisp Publications, 1988.

Montebello, Anthony R. *Work Teams That Work*. Minneapolis: Best Sellers Publishing, 1994.

Peters, Tom. *Liberation Management.* New York: Alfred A. Knopf, 1992.

Peters, Tom, and Robert Waterman, Jr. *In Search of Excellence.* New York: Harper and Row, 1982.

Roman, Mark B. "The Johari Window," *Success,* July–August, 1987.

Zenger, John H., Ed Musselwhite, Kathleen Hurson, and Craig Perrin. *Leading Teams: Mastering the New Role.* Homewood, IL: Business One Irwin, 1994.

Index

Available From SkillPath Publications

Lifelong Learning Library

Practical Project Management: The Secrets of Managing Any Project on Time and on Budget *by Michael Dobson*

Team Power: How to Build and Grow Successful Teams *by Jim Temme*

Self-Study Sourcebooks

Climbing the Corporate Ladder: What You Need to Know and Do to Be a Promotable Person *by Barbara Pachter and Marjorie Brody*

Coping With Supervisory Nightmares: 12 Common Nightmares of Leadership and What You Can Do About Them *by Michael and Deborah Singer Dobson*

Discovering Your Purpose *by Ivy Haley*

Going for the Gold: Winning the Gold Medal for Financial Independence *by Lesley D. Bissett, CFP*

The Innovative Secretary *by Marlene Caroselli, Ed.D.*

Mastering the Art of Communication: Your Keys to Developing a More Effective Personal Style *by Michelle Fairfield Poley*

Organized for Success! 95 Tips for Taking Control of Your Time, Your Space, and Your Life *by Nanci McGraw*

P.E.R.S.U.A.D.E.: Communication Strategies That Move People to Action *by Marlene Caroselli, Ed.D.*

Productivity Power: 250 Great Ideas for Being More Productive *by Jim Temme*

Promoting Yourself: 50 Ways to Increase Your Prestige, Power, and Paycheck *by Marlene Caroselli, Ed.D.*

Risk-Taking: 50 Ways to Turn Risks Into Rewards *by Marlene Caroselli, Ed.D. and David Harris*

Stress Control: How You Can Find Relief From Life's Daily Stress *by Steve Bell*

The Technical Writer's Guide *by Robert McGraw*

Total Quality Customer Service: How to Make It Your Way of Life *by Jim Temme*

Write It Right! A Guide for Clear and Correct Writing *by Richard Andersen and Helene Hinis*

Handbooks

The ABC's of Empowered Teams: Building Blocks for Success *by Mark Towers*

Assert Yourself! Developing Power-Packed Communication Skills to Make Your Points Clearly, Confidently, and Persuasively *by Lisa Contini*

Breaking the Ice: How to Improve Your On-the-Spot Communication Skills
by Deborah Shouse

The Care and Keeping of Customers: A Treasury of Facts, Tips, and Proven
Techniques for Keeping Your Customers Coming BACK! *by Roy Lantz*

Challenging Change: Five Steps for Dealing With Change *by Holly DeForest and
Mary Steinberg*

Dynamic Delegation: A Manager's Guide for Active Empowerment *by Mark Towers*

Every Woman's Guide to Career Success *by Denise M. Dudley*

Great Openings and Closings: 28 Ways to Launch and Land Your Presentations
With Punch, Power, and Pizazz *by Mari Pat Varga*

Hiring and Firing: What Every Manager Needs to Know *by Marlene Caroselli, Ed.D.
with Laura Wyeth, Ms.Ed.*

How to Be a More Effective Group Communicator: Finding Your Role and
Boosting Your Confidence in Group Situations *by Deborah Shouse*

How to Deal With Difficult People *by Paul Friedman*

Learning to Laugh at Work: The Power of Humor in the Workplace
by Robert McGraw

Making Your Mark: How to Develop a Personal Marketing Plan for Becoming
More Visible and More Appreciated at Work *by Deborah Shouse*

Meetings That Work *by Marlene Caroselli, Ed.D.*

The Mentoring Advantage: How to Help Your Career Soar to New Heights
by Pam Grout

Minding Your Business Manners: Etiquette Tips for Presenting Yourself
Professionally in Every Business Situation *by Marjorie Brody
and Barbara Pachter*

Misspeller's Guide *by Joel and Ruth Schroeder*

Motivation in the Workplace: How to Motivate Workers to Peak Performance and
Productivity *by Barbara Fielder*

NameTags Plus: Games You Can Play When People Don't Know What to Say
by Deborah Shouse

Networking: How to Creatively Tap Your People Resources *by Colleen Clarke*

New & Improved! 25 Ways to Be More Creative and More Effective *by Pam Grout*

Power Write! A Practical Guide to Words That Work *by Helene Hinis*

Putting Anger to Work For You! *by Ruth and Joel Schroeder*

Reinventing Your Self: 28 Strategies for Coping With Change *by Mark Towers*

Saying "No" to Negativity: How to Manage Negativity in Yourself, Your Boss, and
Your Co-Workers *by Zoie Kaye*

The Supervisor's Guide: The Everyday Guide to Coordinating People and Tasks
by Jerry Brown and Denise Dudley, Ph.D.

Taking Charge: A Personal Guide to Managing Projects and Priorities
by Michal E. Feder

Treasure Hunt: 10 Stepping Stones to a New and More Confident You!
by Pam Grout

A Winning Attitude: How to Develop Your Most Important Asset!
by Michelle Fairfield Poley

For more information, call 1-800-873-7545.

Notes

Notes